T0198611

Dear Reader,

As a hypnotherapy instructor for many years, I have had the opportunity to instruct students around the world to be hypnotherapists. The one topic that always seems to amaze them is how often they actually go into hypnosis on a daily basis.

From where I sit now, I realize that I have been both the subject as well as the deliverer of hypnotic suggestions most of my life. I realize that I had been hypnotizing thousands of people even before my years as a formal hypnotherapist. I had been doing so in various occupations I held—a U.S. Army drill instructor, a national sales trainer, an ordained minister for many years, and even as a father raising six children.

This book will not only help you to realize how you have been and are being hypnotized on a daily basis, but it will show you how easy it is to effectively take control of this life-changing process and purposefully direct it toward helping you attain your goals now.

The American School of Hypnosis is a hypnosis training center that caters to customers in Massachusetts, New Hampshire, and Maine. Any readers in those areas desiring further formal training through either attending our live, in-person certification classes or home study course should contact us via *www.choosehypnosis.com*. Be sure to mention you purchased this book to receive a substantial 20 percent discount certificate toward your tuition.

Rene Bastarache

The EVERYTHING® Series

These handy, accessible books give you all you need to tackle a difficult project, gain a new hobby, or even brush up on something you learned back in school but have since forgotten. You can read from cover to cover or just pick out information from our four useful boxes.

 Alerts: Urgent warnings

 Essentials: Quick handy tips

 Facts: Important snippets of information

 Questions: Answers to common questions

When you're done reading, you can finally say you know **EVERYTHING**®!

PUBLISHER Karen Cooper

DIRECTOR OF ACQUISITIONS AND INNOVATION Paula Munier

MANAGING EDITOR, EVERYTHING SERIES Lisa Laing

COPY CHIEF Casey Ebert

ACQUISITIONS EDITOR Katie McDonough

DEVELOPMENT EDITOR Brett Palana-Shanahan

EDITORIAL ASSISTANT Hillary Thompson

Visit the entire Everything® series at *www.everything.com*

THE
EVERYTHING®
SELF-
HYPNOSIS
BOOK

Learn to use your mental power
to take control of your life

Rene A. Bastarache, DD,
Founder and Director of
The American School of Hypnosis

Adams Media
New York London Toronto Sydney New Delhi

Adams Media
An Imprint of Simon & Schuster, Inc.
57 Littlefield Street
Avon, Massachusetts 02322

For information about special discounts for bulk purchases, please contact Simon & Schuster Special Sales at 1-866-506-1949 or business@simonand-schuster.com.

The Simon & Schuster Speakers Bureau can bring authors to your live event. For more information or to book an event contact the Simon & Schuster Speakers Bureau at 1-866-248-3049 or visit our website at www.simonspeakers.com.

Manufactured in the United States of America

10 9 8 7 6 5 4 3 2

Library of Congress Cataloging-in-Publication Data has been applied for.

ISBN 978-1-59869-835-0

To my mother Terri for her love and support.

Acknowledgments

I'd like to acknowledge my lovely partner Raluca, who has both assisted me in researching the information for this book as well as inspired me.

Contents

Introduction

Have you ever wished there was a way to quit smoking or lose weight permanently and easily? Have you ever had difficulty sleeping and wished there were an immediate solution? Have you ever wished that you could relax and have better memory retention while taking a test? Have you ever dreamt about having a perfect relationship, being wealthy, and even having great health? While those are some pretty lofty goals, this book can help you take steps in that direction.

All the knowledge that you need to relax, renew your health, eliminate pain, or be successful at any of your desires is already within you. This book will show you how to uncover and utilize that magical power that lies dormant deep within.

All hypnosis is self-hypnosis. You spend the majority of your life in a hypnotizable state. The definition of hypnosis is simply being open to suggestion. You are either open to suggestion or not. You either accept things or you reject them. If you are open to suggestion, you are in a hypnotizable state. That is the basis of hypnosis. The more that you accept and are open to suggestion, the deeper in hypnosis you are. You are being given suggestions constantly in virtually every place you go and everything you do.

This book will teach you how to become aware of the many types of suggestion you are being bombarded with each day. It happens everywhere, from the grocery store, malls, on television and every other form of media, at work, while driving, at school, to family, religion, clubs, the government, and virtually everything else that you participate in.

Once you have become aware of what is happening, you can then take control of what you accept or reject. You will be able to use the power of self-hypnosis to give yourself suggestions in order to progress in attaining your goals.

You will learn many ways to hypnotize yourself easily and permanently. Many of them you are probably doing right now and are just not aware of. You will learn the misconceptions and roadblocks pertaining to hypnosis and how to avoid them. You will be able to condition your thought process to program yourself for success in every area of life including health, wealth, relationships, happiness, and many other topics.

Take the time to study this book and follow the instructions given. You will find that upon completion of this book you will not only have the ability to change virtually any area of your life for the better, but you'll also be able to do the same for the lives of your family, friends, and loved ones.

Chapter 1
All Hypnosis Is Self-Hypnosis

Accepting suggestion in any form is considered hypnosis. It happens when you are listening to positive self-help tapes, reading a fairy tale to your children, listening to the television or radio, having a conversation with a friend over the phone, thumbing through a magazine, or even browsing the newspaper. Since you are accepting the suggestions and allowing them to enter your mind, you are in fact hypnotizing yourself. All hypnosis or suggestion is self-hypnosis.

Have You Been Hypnotized?

Most people upon being asked this question will immediately respond with a resounding no, when, in fact, everyone has been hypnotized before. Most people are being hypnotized on a daily basis and are not even aware of it. Due to the many popular misconceptions, especially those perpetuated by the media, most people do not have a firm or even a slight understanding of what hypnosis actually is. Many think that it is some kind of trance that overtakes them and can make them act like a zombie. Some think it is some mysterious magical power that takes over their self-control and makes them do things against their will.

Fact

> A common technique used by real estate agents to make a house more enticing to prospective clients is to turn on all the lights throughout the house and have the aroma of apple pie wafting through the kitchen. Upon smelling this aroma, clients will immediately regress to the warm, pleasurable memories of having apple pie with grandma.

Grocery Stores

If you have ever gone into a grocery store with the purpose of purchasing ten items and ended up leaving the grocery store having bought fifteen to twenty items, you were a victim of hypnosis. Even though you had a list with you of what items you wanted to purchase, due to the attractive and alluring advertising displays, you were enticed into buying other items by being given the suggestion that they would make you happier or satisfied in some manner. You were enticed by them and purchased them on the spot. When you got home and unpacked your groceries, you may have wondered why you purchased so many additional items you didn't even need. You were open to the suggestion of the products' advertising. That is a very strong form of hypnosis.

When you're hungry this is even more evident. Imagine being hungry and walking in front of the bakery with all the smells of the freshly baked products. There is a strong temptation to purchase something, even if you had not planned on it initially. That is why a grocery store places a bakery within the sight or smell range of the public rather than in the back room.

 Essential

It is important not to go grocery shopping when you are hungry. Create a shopping list of what you intend to purchase and have a snack before leaving the house. When you are hungry you are more open to suggestion, and unhealthy junk foods become much more attractive. Stick to your list as much as you can.

Most grocery stores that utilize food demonstrators will have the demonstrators work during lunch and dinner hours. This technique utilizes the power of suggestion very strongly. During mealtimes you are most likely shopping for what you would like to have for lunch or dinner. You are then confronted by someone who will give you a free sample that is an easy alternative for you and that is already cooked. Upon trying it, especially if you like it, the product is conveniently placed with the cooking instructions right in front of you. If you have ever purchased something in this situation, you have been hypnotized, as the main definition of hypnosis is simply being open to suggestion.

Road Hypnosis

If you have ever driven your car to your destination and then wondered how you got there because you didn't remember driving past some or most of the streets, you were again a victim of hypnosis. This is called road hypnosis. You may have driven that same route hundreds of times to the point where it became a subconscious habit. Since it had become a habit, you did not have to think of the driving directions consciously, and many times you drove subconsciously.

This also happens quite often when you become used to driving to a certain location such as work. You became so used to driving to and from work each and every day that it becomes a habit. Even after changing jobs or moving to another location, many people find themselves subconsciously driving to the old location as a habit.

Positive Affirmations

If you use positive affirmations, then you have been in hypnosis. Positive affirmations are used by many organizations, including many weight loss, smoking cessation, and self-esteem programs. Many of these programs will have you tape affirmations on the walls, mirrors, and other strategic places where you spend most of your time so you can read them throughout the day. Even if you do not read them directly, the affirmations work on you subliminally as they can be seen through your peripheral vision.

Music

Music is also very hypnotic. The music you listen to can greatly enhance your mood. There are very positive, uplifting songs that can raise your vibrations to a very happy positive state, and there are also negative songs with lyrics that can drag you down, create anger, and instill hostility.

Have you ever taken the time to listen to the lyrics of your favorite songs? If not, make a point to do so in the near future. You may be surprised as to what you have been listening to and what messages you have been giving your subconscious mind. Even though you may have simply been listening to the melody and not paying attention to the words, it is important to realize that the subconscious mind absorbs everything all the time. It doesn't miss a trick. It is capable of doing unlimited tasks simultaneously. Take the time to see what messages you are giving yourself.

What Is Hypnosis?

When you take a moment to think about what hypnosis is, the first picture that comes to mind for many people is a sinister Svengali character, all dressed in black with a long trench coat, a goatee, and evil eyes. You picture this evil character with both of his hands up in the air, fingers pointing at the subject with hypnotic rays emanating from his fingertips commanding the subject to obey.

Although this is the image that comes to mind for most, it is merely fiction. Hypnosis has nothing to do with sinister hypnotists being in control of you or possessing any magical powers.

The Reality

What is hypnosis exactly? To be specific would be rather difficult as there are many differences of opinion in the scientific and medical communities as to what actually takes place. This has been a subject of controversy for over 200 years and is as difficult to answer as it would be in understanding the complexities of the human mind itself.

The word *hypnosis* derives from the Greek word for sleep, *hypnos*, which is also the name of the Greek god of sleep. Although the actual state of hypnosis is very different from sleep, it is often confused with sleep as many people who are in hypnosis find it to be extremely relaxing.

Hypnosis covers such a wide variety of topics and practices that it can be difficult to determine exactly where hypnosis starts and where it ends. There are, however, several theories that may shed light on the workings of hypnosis. The following methods are commonly used within the medical, mental health, and hypnotic communities and will explain hypnosis more clearly.

Suggestibility

One theory is that hypnosis is a trancelike state where the subject is extremely open to suggestion. In many cases the subject is relaxed almost to the point of sleep. This, in fact, is one of the most commonly used definitions of hypnosis.

 Essential

Hollywood is notorious for portraying people under hypnosis as in a trance or like zombies. One famous movie features a character named Svengali, a sinister, villainous hypnotist who takes advantage of young women. Svengali was initially a character in the romantic novel *Trilby*, which was written in 1894.

If you think about the definition of hypnosis as being open to suggestion, you will realize that throughout your day you are either open to or resisting suggestion. There are no other options. Therefore, if you are not fighting suggestion, then you are open to suggestion and in a hypnotized state.

Deep Relaxation

Another common theory of hypnosis is that it is a state of deep relaxation. It is a deep feeling of "losing yourself" to your relaxation. You are aware of what's going on around you. Although deep relaxation is a part of hypnosis, it is not a complete definition as to how it works. In addition to being relaxed, you can also be hypnotized while walking, reading, working on the computer, or even while you are in pain. Obviously when you are in pain you are not in a relaxed state. You can even be in a frantic, out-of-control state and still be brought into hypnosis.

Imagination and Focused Attention

One of the key ingredients in hypnosis is the use of your imagination. The more you can focus your imagination and concentration, the more effective hypnosis will be for you. An important factor to realize is that the subconscious mind gives the same value to real and imagined memories. Therefore, if you can use your imagination and focus on what you want long enough, your subconscious will eventually believe that it has happened and will look at it as reality.

It has been proven scientifically through quantum physics that thoughts are energy and can become reality if dwelt upon. An example of this would be thinking of a cold winter's day even though it is warm outside, and as you imagine the cold you actually begin to get chilly. If you can imagine your goal, then it is attainable; if you cannot imagine it, then it is out of your reach.

Altered State of Mind

Hypnosis is also frequently described as an altered state of mind. Although what constitutes an altered state of mind is not exactly defined, hypnosis has been associated with altered brain wave states. Therefore, being in any brain wave state that is not of the waking or beta state could constitute being in an altered state of mind. Brain waves will be thoroughly discussed in Chapter 6.

Confusion Technique

Another theory of hypnosis is that through confusing or keeping the conscious mind busy, you can bypass the critical thinking of the conscious mind and thereby directly influence the subconscious mind with positive suggestions.

 Essential

Most everyone has experienced hypnosis at one time or another, especially when sitting in class at school. If you have ever found yourself daydreaming during a class, you were in hypnosis. Just as daydreaming can be controlled, you can give yourself suggestions while daydreaming to effect positive change.

This is similar to trying to do your taxes while having a conversation with someone at the same time. In order to complete your taxes properly, you would have to disengage from the conversation. Once you have done so and continue to work on your taxes, everything that is being said by the person who is speaking goes directly into your subconscious mind without the hindrance of the critical conscious mind, which is kept busy concentrating on the taxes.

Hypnosis Is Everywhere

Hypnosis is constantly being used in television commercials. Have you ever watched a television commercial and at the end of it felt like you needed that product? Or maybe even you pick up the phone to call the number for a product that was advertised on the TV screen. Television commercials suggest (sometimes not so subtly) that you need a certain product, and if it's a well-made commercial, it will even give you the suggestion that you need it right now. It will suggest to you that supplies are limited and you must pick up the phone and call right this very moment. Television ads use many forms of coercion. They lead you to believe that operators are standing by, that you must purchase a product now or you'll lose your opportunity forever, that millions of other shoppers have purchased it and are in the smart or popular group, and even if you are not satisfied they will give you double your money back and you can keep the free gift for yourself. If you are in a frame of mind that is open to suggestion, these promises can be very alluring.

Television advertising, in addition to convincing you how great a product is or how popular you will be if you purchase it, will also prey on your fears. Some of the most successful and popular advertising campaigns on television today are from pharmaceutical companies. These commercials ask if you have experienced any one of a myriad of symptoms that could cover pretty much anybody who breathes. Then once they have stated all of the symptoms that you may have, they conveniently mention that they have the solution for your problems in a pill that is supposedly a miracle drug for these symptoms. Then they urge you to call your doctor and tell him that you need this pill. It's amazing that, as a result of these commercials, patients are calling their doctors and asking for a certain pill to cure their self-diagnosis.

 Alert!

It is extremely important that you are vigilant as to what information enters into your subconscious. When you hear these conditioning commercials, immediately eliminate the negative suggestions. Whatever input your subconscious receives on a continual basis will become fact, even if it is from a commercial stating that you will be sick unless you buy a certain product.

You are also being hypnotized on a daily basis through radio, billboards, magazines, and virtually any place else where there is advertising. You have been hypnotized your entire life through suggestions from your family, school, government, church, military, work, and any other type of group that you attend. It happens any time that your thought process is changed, enhanced, or coerced.

Hypnosis can be found everywhere in virtually every walk of life. Think about the major conditioning sources in your life: school, religion, government, television, military, and family. Each one attempts to teach you or lead you in a certain way of believing or thinking. Some of these organizations condition you to slant your thinking toward their agenda or purpose.

Fact

> The educational system also teaches through repetition. By being open to suggestion you are able to learn. The things that you learn stay with you throughout your life and become part of your belief system. You in turn impart this same knowledge to your children.

Who Can Be Hypnotized?

Most people seem to think that they cannot be hypnotized. The reason for this is due to the many misconceptions that are portrayed by the media about hypnosis.

Reasonable Intelligence

Anyone with reasonable intelligence can be hypnotized. That statement usually raises a few eyebrows. What is meant by "reasonable intelligence" is anyone who can follow simple instructions. If you were given instructions to the store across the street and were able to follow them, you could also be hypnotized.

Exceptions to Hypnosis

In most cases, if you are able to understand the language in which the suggestions are being given, then you can be hypnotized. Oftentimes very young children cannot be hypnotized because of their lack of ability to follow simple instructions or sit still while being given suggestions.

 Alert!

Young children may not be able to be hypnotized in a traditional manner as they are so full of energy and have difficulty sitting still and paying attention. These young children can still be hypnotized through a process known as *sleep hypnosis*, where they are given suggestions when they are between the waking and sleep states.

People with severe mental disabilities cannot be hypnotized because they are not able to understand the suggestions that are given; however, there are always exceptions to this rule. Once again, as long as they are able to understand you and follow your instructions, they can be hypnotized.

Resistance

Even though anyone with reasonable intelligence who can follow simple instructions can be hypnotized, it is important to realize that anyone can also resist hypnosis if he or she chooses. While in hypnosis, you are under your own control and not that of the hypnotist; therefore, if you are given a suggestion to do something that you do not like, you would simply choose to not do it. No matter what the suggestion is or how deep in hypnosis you may be, you will always have the ability to resist.

Types of Hypnosis

Once you understand the nature of hypnosis as simply being open to suggestion, you'll realize that hypnosis can be used to improve virtually any area of your life. It can be used on individuals as well as large groups. It can be successfully utilized over the telephone, television, radio, or even over a computer. Here are a few of the main venues where hypnosis has been found to be very successful.

Self-Hypnosis

All hypnosis is self-hypnosis. Whenever suggestions are being given, if you are open to the suggestions, then you are accepting them. Whether you are hypnotizing yourself, hypnotizing others, listening to suggestions of others, or even reading an interesting book, if you are open to suggestions then you are utilizing self-hypnosis.

Clinical Hypnosis

Hypnosis can be used to help you improve in virtually any area of your life where improvement is required. With clinical hypnosis, the power of suggestion is used to help people for a wide range of topics, from smoking cessation all the way to pain management, memory retention, the elimination of phobias and panic attacks, and even for recoding negative emotions or feelings. Clinical hypnosis is a very effective tool to bypass the conscious mind and effect positive changes through suggestion.

Group Hypnosis

While group hypnosis is not as effective as clinical hypnosis or an individual session, group hypnosis is a more affordable choice to receive positive suggestions. Most group sessions are done for topics such as smoking cessation, weight loss, stress reduction, and even metaphysical practices such as past-life regression and contacting spirits. The advantage of group sessions is that you are in attendance with others, which in many cases makes people feel more comfortable. Individual sessions can be tailored to the client, whereas a group session can only be delivered in one specific way. Hopefully the way that the hypnosis session is delivered will be effective for most of the participants in attendance.

Comedy Hypnosis

This is a very interesting phenomenon in the realm of hypnosis. If you have never had the opportunity to experience a comedy hypnosis show, it is well worth your time to attend one. It is a very good demonstration of what can be done with hypnosis, and it is also extremely entertaining.

With comedy hypnosis, the volunteers onstage are asked to perform a variety of things for the purpose of entertainment and showing the limits of hypnosis. Through suggestibility, the volunteers are led through many skits, such as acting like chickens, dancing the ballet, forgetting their own names, and regressing to being very young children.

 Fact

In a comedy hypnosis show, subjects volunteer because they want to look silly in front of their friends. The hypnotist tests the volunteers, and the least desirable candidates are asked to return to their seats. Now when the volunteers are asked to act like chickens, the hypnotist knows he will get the best chickens.

As a result of watching a comedy hypnosis show, many people in the audience find it hard to believe that these volunteers are actually in hypnosis. Many times they feel that they are just play-acting or doing whatever they are doing to entertain the crowd. The truth of the matter is that the people who participate in a comedy stage show are in a deeper level of hypnosis than they would be if participating in a clinical hypnosis session. For most clinical hypnosis sessions, participants are only required to be in the lighter states of hypnosis. For most of the skits that are performed in a comedy show, participants are in a deeper level of hypnosis. In order to experience hallucinations or even what is known as *negative hallucinations* (not seeing something that is there), you must be in the very deepest stages of hypnosis. This is the same level of hypnosis that you are in for anesthesia.

Forensic Hypnosis

Forensic hypnosis is an extremely interesting field and is very effective. It is important to realize that every sound, sight, taste, smell, and anything you have experienced since the day you were born, whether it is right in front of you or even through your peripheral vision, is logged in perfect clarity in your subconscious mind. With the use of forensic hypnosis, this information can be accessed. By being able to access this cache of information, many questions can be answered. Forensic hypnosis can be used to help identify specific information required from a hit-and-run accident or many other types of witnessed crimes. It can even be used to help someone find lost objects.

How Hypnosis Can Work for You

The ways that you can use hypnosis to help yourself or to improve the lives of others are unlimited. As long as you are open-minded, have a true desire to improve, and are committed to your goal, it can work for you. Here are just a few of the ways that hypnosis can benefit you.

Eliminating Bad Habits

This is probably one of the most frequent uses of hypnosis. In most clinical hypnosis offices, smoking cessation and weight loss account for approximately 75 percent of their business.

Although smoking is an addiction, it can be very successfully eliminated through the assistance of hypnosis. Remembering that you cannot be hypnotized against your will, you must have a desire to quit smoking for hypnosis to work. Hypnosis is a wonderful helpmate but not a magic spell.

Weight loss is also commonly treated with hypnosis. While the amount of weight loss each week with hypnosis may be less than many of the fad diets on the market today, it is a gradual, safe way to lose weight. Many additional suggestions can be given during a weight-loss session, such as increasing metabolism, energy, exercise, and the desire to eat healthy foods; eating slower; and eating much less.

Other bad habits that are very commonly addressed with hypnosis are nail biting, bedwetting, and laziness, which, if the subject has the desire to change, can be handled very easily. Many people are also finding hypnosis to be extremely helpful in dealing with anger issues and in controlling their tempers.

Ease Pain and Heal Faster

In addition to eliminating bad habits, hypnosis has also been found very effective in dealing with healing and pain management. Many of the more open-minded hospitals are now including hypnotherapists on their staff. Hospitals are realizing that hypnotherapy can be a viable alternative to anesthesia as well as aid their patients in healing faster.

 Alert!

It is important to realize that pain is a signal that the body utilizes to inform you that something is wrong. Before treating yourself or others for pain, it is important to have a medical professional review the source of the pain to ensure the safety of the person.

Hypnosis is extensively used in childbirth. Hypnotic child-birthing clinics are springing up all over the country as an alternative to traditional birthing centers or hospitals. Through the hypnotic birthing process, a woman is able to experience less painful childbirth, and, depending on her suggestibility, may find it to be quite an enjoyable experience. The advantages to hypnotic birthing are that it is much less stressful on the child, and it helps to accelerate the healing and recuperation of the mother and the child. This is a wonderful alternative to using anesthesia.

Another medical area where hypnosis has been extremely successful is in working with patients with severe pain. With the assistance of hypnosis, patients are able to bring themselves or be brought by a hypnotherapist to a state of extreme relaxation. Hypnosis can also be used to help them have a positive mindset and even to increase strength or energy, which aids in the healing process.

Business

Hypnosis and the business community have turned out to be a wonderful match. Most highly successful corporations have been sending their top salespeople or managers to sales and motivation training for years. They have found that if they can improve their employees' self-images through many of the motivational techniques that are taught, in the long run it will increase their productivity as well as their income-earning potential.

Through hypnosis you can greatly enhance someone's sales ability, public speaking ability, productivity, confidence, assertiveness, attitude, and the list goes on and on.

Eliminate Fears

There has been an extremely high success rate in dealing with phobias and panic attacks utilizing hypnosis. With hypnosis you are able to get to the root cause of a phobia and either eliminate the cause or change the way you look at or feel about it, thereby eliminating the fear. Hypnosis is used to address some of the most common phobias, such as fear of spiders, flying, bridges, needles, exam anxiety, dogs, going places, driving, and socializing.

Personal Issues

Hypnosis can greatly help many personal areas in your life. Self-improvement suggestions can be given for success motivation, attaining goals, increasing confidence, and building a positive mental attitude. Other areas of self-improvement that are very popular as well as successful with hypnosis are in enjoying life and being happy.

There are also many relationship issues that can be addressed with hypnosis. Suggestions can be given to help you improve your patience or tolerance, be more considerate, eliminate selfishness, work as a team, increase understanding, and even be more loving and attentive. In the area of breakups, it can greatly help ease your ex-partner from your mind by increasing your self-confidence so you can move on with your life.

Chapter 2
How the Mind Functions

If you were to look at the human brain, you would see an organ that seems to be made up of many different parts. The most obvious are the two symmetrical portions on the right and left sides. Each part of the brain has entirely different functions; however, they all work in synchronicity with each other.

Are You in Your "Right" Mind?

The two symmetrical portions of the brain are known as *hemispheres*. They are simply called the left hemisphere and the right hemisphere, or left brain and right brain. Each hemisphere is responsible for different modes of thinking. It is interesting to note that everyone prefers or utilizes one hemisphere more than the other. Both hemispheres are connected by a group of nerves called the *corpus callosum*. This is how the two sides receive input from each other.

The right brain controls the left side of the body, and the left brain controls the right side of the body. The sides of the brain are entirely different in the way that they take in information. Many times this difference can cause confusion in the decision-making process of the conscious mind.

As newborns, babies have not created a preference over which way they are going to think, and neither of the hemispheres has been developed more than the other. However, once the baby has begun to grow and develop and receives any type of formal education, the child will usually begin to develop one side of the brain over the other. Since the educational system is mainly geared toward left-brain thinking, in most cases the left hemisphere of the brain becomes more developed than the right. As a result, children who utilize more left-brain activity usually do better in school.

Left Brain

The left half of the brain is where speech and many other important skills dealing with logic and reasoning come from. This is the part of the brain that is in control of the right side of your body. Anything that is familiar is acknowledged by the left brain. It is the analytical and judgmental part of your mind.

 Fact

These are characteristics of the left brain: logical, sequential, rational, analytical, objective, looks at the parts, detailed, facts oriented, present and past, math and science, comprehension, acknowledges, patterns, perceptions, reality based, forms strategies, practical, verbal, linear processing, and perceptive.

The types of activities that are associated with left-brained individuals are problem-solving activities such as assembling puzzles, language usage activities, utilizing math or geometry, and recognition and analytical activities such as playing chess and categorizing things.

Left-brain people are able to follow rules exactly as stated, without deviation. They are in their comfort zone when they have clearly stated directions to follow, and when there are none they will create instructions or parameters for themselves. Left-brain individuals are very logical and like things to be spelled out for them in detail. They have difficulty when trying to understand vague or abstract ideas. When things are not clear they become confused. They express themselves easily with words and are extremely articulate and literal in what they say. They like everything to be proven and matter of fact.

Right Brain

The right brain is the more creative and emotional part of the brain. It is the part of the brain that controls the left side of the body. The right brain deals with anything that is new or not familiar. It concerns itself with the present and the future and is very creative in its outlook.

 Fact

> These are characteristics of the right brain: random, intuitive, holistic, athletic, emotional, artistic, subjective, looks at whole or the big picture, imaginative, symbols and images, present and future, philosophy and religion, believes, appreciates, fantasy based, presents possibilities, and risk taking.

The right brain looks at the big picture rather than the individual details. It takes in information in large pieces or chunks. (It is the duty of the left brain to then take that information and break it down.) The right brain is very visual and is responsible for creative imagery and imagination. The types of activities that are associated with the right brain are creative activities involving anything having to do with seeing, feeling, imagination, visualization, colors, sizes, and smells. Things having to do with faith, spiritualism, holistics, or the future are based in the right brain.

A way to encourage right-brained students would be to have them work in groups or use other creative methods of learning such as projects, games, or anything that requires creativity. Other techniques that can be used for teaching right-brained students include visual aids, role-playing, storytelling, and analogies.

Alert!

In attending a left-brain type lecture, a right-brained student may find it helpful to take notes, make diagrams, and even create drawings of what is being taught. Right-brain students will also find it advantageous to create study groups with other right-brain students to discuss the day's lesson.

The functions of the two parts of the brain are not clearly designated. Each can do the other's work, just not as efficiently. Most people have a tendency to lean toward using the left or right brain while thinking or learning. For instance, right-brain-dominated people are often poor spellers as they tend to rely more on their intuition rather than actually studying the order in which the letters in a word occur.

Conflict from Within

Although it would be wonderful if you could use both sides of your brain simultaneously, in reality only one side can be utilized at a time. In most cases it is the left brain that will ultimately win the conflict, thereby creating an imbalance within the mind.

Since the left brain assumes a position of dominance, it can be difficult for both sides of the brain to become equally as developed, thereby stunting the growth of the right brain. There are ways to shut down or mask the left brain temporarily to give the right brain time to function. One of the most effective ways to do this is by boring the left brain through techniques such as meditation, deep relaxation, or self-hypnosis.

During these relaxation techniques, the left brain seems to step off to the side so that the imagination and creativity of the right brain can transfer its information to the conscious mind. Unfortunately, in this busy world that we live in where the left brain is dominant and there is little time to simply meditate or relax, the right brain often does not have enough time to develop and thereby expresses its creativity primarily in the dreaming and day-dreaming states.

The Conscious Mind

The conscious mind encompasses approximately 5 percent of the brain and operates very similarly to the left brain. The conscious mind is the portion of the brain that is in control at all times, the command center.

Creature of Habit

If you would like things to turn out any differently than they have in the past, then you must do something different, which requires change. The conscious mind rebels against this type of behavior. Obviously, the conscious mind wants to improve, but it wants to do so without having to change anything.

 Essential

The conscious mind is a creature of habit. It does not like to be inconvenienced in any way and enjoys remaining the same (the status quo). It rebels against anything new, even if it involves positive change. This is an important feature to be aware of since self-improvement requires change.

This is where the dilemma lies with people who have difficulty in changing a habit such as smoking or overeating. They want to create a new habit of health, and consciously they know exactly what needs to be done to accomplish their goal. The one thing that seems to stand in their way is their conscious mind. They may begin the process to change and even make progress but suddenly will fall back to old habits.

Geared Negatively

Another feature of the conscious mind is that it is geared negatively. Imagine someone you have never met before approaching you and telling you that you are the most intelligent person that he has ever met and that your sense of fashion and style is amazing. Your first response may be, "What's this guy trying to sell me?" Even though this stranger may have been very sincere with his compliment, the conscious mind looks for an alternative motive; it is suspicious.

Literal Behavior

The conscious mind operates mostly within the beta brain wave frequency state (more on this in Chapter 6). It is more analytical in nature and sees things as they are literally. It is the part of the mind that figures things out through reasoning, logic, and common sense. It sees things as black and white rather than abstract. It is the part of the mind that tends to be judgmental and analytical.

The Subconscious Mind

The subconscious mind is the remaining 95 percent of the mind, and it operates very similarly to the right brain. It is the information center for the conscious mind. If the conscious mind is similar to the keyboard and monitor of a computer, then the subconscious would be the hard drive. It is your long-term memory and storage.

Your Hard Drive

The purpose for the subconscious mind is solely to collect information. It takes in every bit of input whether it is positive or negative. It does not make judgments over the information that it collects since that is the responsibility of the conscious mind. Every sight, sound, taste, smell, or anything you've experienced since the day that you were born is stored in your subconscious mind for future retrieval.

Once anything becomes a habit, it becomes part of the subconscious mind. If you take a few moments to think about it, you will see that there are many things that you do subconsciously. In fact, anything that you do repeatedly eventually becomes a habit and will become a subconscious activity.

Many people recite the alphabet subconsciously. If you were to recite the alphabet as quickly as possible, it would likely take about six to seven seconds. Now if you were to recite only half of the alphabet, it would seem to make sense that it should only take half the time that it took to recite the entire alphabet. Try to do it now, but only recite every other letter. It takes longer, but why? When you recited the entire alphabet, you were able to do it quickly since it is a subconscious habit; it was something that you didn't even have to think about. However, when you recited half the alphabet, you now had to consciously think of each letter and vocally skip over every other one.

You compute simple math problems subconsciously. Here's an example: answer these questions to yourself very quickly. What is 2×2? What is $3 + 3$? What is 5×2? What is the square root of 2,325? You'll find that the first three questions were most likely answered subconsciously (automatically) since you use them so often in life. However, the fourth one, if you were able to answer it at all, required conscious effort. You may have even had to refer to a math table or use a pencil and paper to figure it out.

There is much information stored within the subconscious mind. Many times if you are not sure exactly how things should be, your subconscious mind can do a scan of the information available and similar past experiences for the answer. It has the ability to fill in the blank or make a guesstimate of how things should be.

 Fact

Other things that you do subconsciously are recall your telephone number, address, date of birth, and your Social Security number. When you use a computer or a typewriter and touch-type, you are typing subconsciously. Otherwise, you would be thinking of every single letter as you typed it and it would take much longer.

Here is an example of this remarkable feature of the mind. Read through the following paragraph and see if you are able to make sense of it.

Yuor mnid has a uqiue alibity to be albe to raed wdors eevn if tehy are not speleld coretcrly. Tihs is one of the mian resaons why you shulod not eidt yuor own wrok. As lnog as msot of the wrod is speleld coretcrly, scuh as the frsit and the lsat lteter, the sucbconsouis can usullay fugire out the rset on its own. The raseon for tihs is taht wehn you raed, you do not look at erevy lteter. You sacn thurogh the wrods and yuor mnid fugires out the rset. Ins't tihs a reamkrable alibity?

The Four-Year-Old Child

The subconscious mind is similar to a four-year-old child. It is innocent, naive, and wants to help you in any way it can but has no idea how. The subconscious mind will try to help, but it does not always make the best choices. Say you were in a severe car accident. The subconscious mind might try to protect you by giving you panic attacks any time you try to leave your house. Its logic may be that if you do not leave the house, you will not get in another car accident.

Four Subconscious Rules to Remember

There are four major rules that the subconscious mind follows. Understanding these will greatly help you on your path to self-improvement. Keep in mind while reading these rules that the subconscious mind reacts similarly to a very young child.

Rule 1—It Does Exactly as the Conscious Mind States

This would be a wonderful feature if the conscious mind would always make the best decisions. Unfortunately, since the conscious mind is a creature of habit, in many instances it does not make the proper decisions. Therefore, even though you want to progress in a certain area, if your conscious mind is continually fighting change, which is its nature, the subconscious will not change.

Rule 2—It Does Not Understand the Concept of Negative

The subconscious mind does not respond or react to words; it responds to pictures and emotions. Wherever you place your thoughts, focus, and emotions, your subconscious mind will respond. People who have a desire to change, rather than thinking about what they do want, often focus on what they don't want. Rather than focusing on being healthy, they focus on not wanting to be sick. Rather than focusing on having a great relationship, they focus on not breaking up. Since the focus is on the negative rather than the positive, they end up attracting to their lives more of what they don't want.

Rule 3—It Does Not Have a Sense of Humor

Think about some of the humorous phrases or idioms that you use on a daily basis. Now imagine stating these phrases to a four-year-old child. Do you think she would understand exactly what you mean? Remember, the subconscious mind takes everything that the conscious mind says literally.

Here are a few statements that people say on a daily basis. As you read them, think about how well a four-year-old child would understand them. "He's so funny that it drives me crazy." "He knocks my socks off." "Doesn't he just kill you?" It is important to be literal while speaking and mean exactly what you say. Keep in mind that whatever you say, at any time of the day, your subconscious mind is responding with, "Make it so!"

Rule 4—It Does Not Understand Sarcasm

Sarcasm is another type of speech that your four-year-old child within does not understand. You will be much more effective with your speech if you can avoid sarcasm totally. There is actually no positive or redeeming feature in utilizing sarcasm. For the most part it is simply a humorous way to say something negative or insulting. Take a moment to think of any statements that you say on a regular basis that may be sarcastic. If you said them to a four-year-old, would the statements be understood the way that you meant them to be?

Seeing the Big Picture

You now have an understanding of how your mind works. If you understand the qualities of the conscious and the subconscious mind, you're better able to understand why you often do the things that you do. But there is still one piece of the puzzle that is missing: how to change this behavior that is natural to you.

The British Guard

Imagine your conscious mind as a British guard, one of those beefeaters guarding Buckingham Palace, standing at attention in full uniform with a rifle guarding the door to your subconscious mind. Anything that attempts to enter your subconscious, such as suggestions, will be immediately challenged by this guard. Even though you want to improve yourself, the conscious mind will challenge any suggestion that requires change.

If you decided that you would like to quit smoking and continually bombarded your mind with positive suggestions to quit, your conscious mind will rebel against each suggestion. Your conscious mind may rationalize that it will be all right to continue smoking, that cigarettes don't cost too much, that even though you get tired often you'll get better soon, and may even go as far as to tell you not to worry about cancer because you'll never get it.

Your Nature

The conscious mind is in command of the subconscious. It is important to remember that the conscious mind is a creature of habit with a rather negative disposition. Whenever positive suggestions for change are given, it has a tendency to be critical of them and ultimately reject them.

The subconscious mind, you'll recall, is similar to an innocent, naive, four-year-old child that wants to help you anyway it can but has no idea how. It has all the information and power at its fingertips to be able to change or enhance virtually any area of your life. The subconscious will do exactly as the conscious mind states, if there were only a way to get the conscious mind to want to do the proper thing. Herein lies the problem.

The Challenge

It is important to realize that in order to progress in any area of life that you are not presently progressing in, or to change your behavior, you must do something different from what you are doing now. In other words, change requires doing something different or being inconvenienced. The more that you can stretch your limits, the more you will progress. Since the conscious mind is a creature of habit, you must find a way to bypass the conscious with positive suggestions so the subconscious may react to them.

The Solution

The solution to this problem is where the strong power of suggestion comes into play. Through the power of suggestion, you are able to relax the conscious mind or take the rebelliousness away from it so that the subconscious will react to positive suggestions. With the rebelliousness of the conscious mind out of the way, the subconscious mind will react immediately to whatever suggestions it is given.

 Essential

If you continue to do the same things for the next five years that you have done for the last five years, five years from now you will be in the same place that you are today. It's interesting to see how many people will continue doing the exact same thing day after day expecting to see different results.

For example, if you seem to be consciously rebelling against quitting smoking, you still know that it is something that you want to do. Once you are able to relax or eliminate the rebellious nature of the conscious mind and then give positive suggestions about quitting smoking, you will react to the suggestion unless it is against your nature. Of course, since you want to quit smoking, the suggestion to quit smoking is not against your nature or your personal standards, and it will be reacted on immediately. That is where the strength of utilizing the subconscious mind comes from. Remember, 95 percent of your mind is subconscious and only 5 percent is conscious, so once the subconscious is given the okay, its ability to change is so much stronger than the conscious mind.

In order to create a positive change in your life, the one key ingredient that is required is *change*. Since the conscious mind is a creature of habit and rebels against change, you are actually challenging yourself to improve. In order to win the challenge you must bypass the conscious mind, the guard. Once you have bypassed your rebellious nature, using one of the many techniques that you will learn in this book, your ability to change will be achieved.

Ways to Bypass the Mind

There are four basic ways to bypass the conscious mind and deliver positive suggestions to the subconscious. Here are the four basic methods with a brief description of each.

Relaxation

The most common way to get suggestions past the conscious mind into the subconscious is through deep relaxation. By relaxing the conscious mind you are decreasing its negative nature, and the positive suggestions are able to bypass it and go into the subconscious. This technique works on the majority of people. You will learn much more of the details of this concept in the next chapter.

Keep It Busy

Some people are not able to relax or do not enjoy relaxing as much as others. For these people (who are a small portion of society), their minds must be kept busy for suggestions to get through. Once given a job to do, they will focus their entire attention on the job, thereby letting down their conscious guard. Once that has been accomplished, the suggestions can slip by the conscious mind into the subconscious.

Shock It

The third way of bypassing the conscious mind is by using rapid or instant induction. Rapid or instant inductions are most often used during comedy hypnosis shows. This is an instantaneous form of hypnosis in which the hypnotist, through one of many methods, shouts the word "sleep" and the subject appears to immediately drop into a deep hypnotic trance. A very effective area of rapid or instant inductions is emergency hypnosis, which is often used by EMTs and other training emergency personnel.

The basic concept of instant or rapid induction is to bypass the conscious mind by shocking it for several seconds. If you ever while sleeping felt that you were on the edge of your bed and suddenly began to fall, you have experienced an instant induction. For one or two seconds you feel as if you are trying to catch your balance and doing everything within your power to not fall. At that very same time in which you are trying to catch your balance consciously, if a one-word suggestion such as "sleep" or "heal" were given, it would immediately bypass the conscious mind and be reacted upon by the subconscious.

Fact

Faith-healing ministries frequently use instant induction. The healer places his hand on the forehead of the person to be healed while his eyes are closed, and the healer shouts the word "heal" as he pushes the subject all the way down to the ground. In this case, "heal" is substituted for the word "sleep."

Returning to the analogy of the British guard standing in front of your subconscious, a rapid induction would be like walking beside the guard as he was looking straight ahead and suddenly, without warning, pushing him away from the door. At the split second that you pushed him and he was trying to catch his balance, you would immediately run through the door into the subconscious mind. By the time the guard caught his balance and got back to the door, the suggestion had already succeeded in making its way through.

Medications

Medications are often used in hospital emergency and operating rooms. Patients under anesthesia are highly susceptible to suggestions. This is why it is very important while someone is undergoing a medical procedure that they be given positive suggestions toward healing and success. Many hospitals throughout the country are now aware of this and as a result will play soothing music in the operating rooms. Many hospitals use video or audio recording devices to ensure that medical personnel are not saying anything negative during the procedure that can hinder the recuperation of patients. When under anesthesia, whatever suggestion the doctor gives will be reacted upon by the subconscious mind.

Chapter 3
How Suggestible Are You?

Are you open to suggestion or not? You may be the type of person who is calm, laid back, and easily accepts every suggestion that is given to you. On the other hand, you may be the type of person who does not enjoy relaxing and tends to be more critical about accepting positive suggestions. In this chapter you will learn how to tell which one of these categories you fall into so you can determine the most productive way to hypnotize yourself.

Have an Open Mind

In order to benefit from hypnosis you must have an open mind. In other words, you must *want* to be affected by hypnosis in order for anything to take place. During the process of hypnosis, nothing happens by itself. It is not a mysterious outside force overtaking your mind and making you do strange things that you have no control over. It is entirely based on suggestion.

Acceptance

How open to suggestion are you? The more open that you are, the more accepting you are of suggestion, the stronger the effect will be. It is similar to having a doctor standing on the front steps of your house. In order for her to help you, you must open the door and let her in. Unless you do that, she will remain on the front doorstep completely useless. She cannot help you unless you allow her to.

Degree of Acceptance

What is your degree of suggestibility? Are you 100 percent open or is there a small degree of resistance hiding somewhere that you do not want to face? People are often open to suggestion; however, there is some resistance that holds them back from being helped with their situation. Imagine you are a civil servant and you need to pass an exam to get a better paying job. Even though the job pays better than what you are making now, you enjoy your present job and have reservations about whether you will enjoy the promotion. Although all of the information needed to pass the test is stored within your subconscious mind, you still fail the test because there is a degree of resistance that will not allow you to recover that information. You failed the test because on a subconscious level that is what you really wanted.

Resistance to Change

This resistance can be seen oftentimes with people who have a desire to quit smoking. They go to the hypnotherapist saying that they are 100 percent committed to quitting; however, when the hypnotherapist asks them to turn in all of their cigarettes and cigarette-related paraphernalia, their faces turn pale. All of a sudden the reality hits them that they are there to quit smoking permanently. At this point the wall of resistance begins to show itself.

 Question?

How much of a commitment should someone have to change?

On a scale of one to ten, one being the least amount of commitment as if it really didn't matter and ten being the highest amount as if you believed it was your last possible resort, where would you put your commitment or desire to change? If you cannot say seven or above, then you may not be committed enough.

It is important to realize that resistance is in opposition to suggestibility. Before choosing to hypnotize yourself, for whatever topic, be sure that you are 100 percent open to make the change. Is there any resistance, fear, or rebellion keeping you from obtaining this goal? If there is, you may want to take some time to address these issues and eliminate them.

An Analytical Approach

People who do not like to relax are categorized as analytical. They account for 20 percent of society. These are the people who say, "I will relax later," but later never seems to come. They are the ones who enjoy keeping busy most of the time. In order to get suggestions past the conscious mind of an analytical person, you must keep his mind busy. Remember the doing your taxes and having a conversation analogy from Chapter 1. You have to let go of one thing or the other. If the conscious mind lets go of the conversation to focus on doing the taxes, the conversation (which is still going on) will bypass the conscious guard and enter directly into the subconscious mind without resistance. If you are predominantly analytical, all you need to do is give yourself a job to do to keep your mind busy, and any positive suggestions given by someone else or a tape recorder while your mind is busy will immediately enter and be accepted by your subconscious mind.

Suggestions, Not Commands

It is important to realize that, whether you are relaxed or your mind is busy, you still have the ability to reject a suggestion at any time even though the suggestion was able to bypass the conscious mind. Even though the conscious mind is engaged and its resistance is down, it still hears everything that is being said. So if the suggestion being given is against the nature or standards of your conscious mind, you will still be able to negate the suggestion. This is why they are called suggestions and not commands. You always have the choice to accept or reject a suggestion no matter how deep you are in hypnosis, and you can never be made to do anything against your will.

Fact

It is important to realize that no one is 100 percent analytical or nonanalytical. Everyone falls somewhere between those two extremes. Even if you may have tested as analytical according to suggestibility, you still have parts of you that may behave in a non-analytical manner in some situations.

The Nonanalytical Approach

People who are able to relax easily while they are doing any type of task are categorized as nonanalytical. They account for approximately 80 percent of society. They are the people who seem to enjoy themselves no matter what they are doing. In order to get suggestions past the conscious mind with a nonanalytical person, all you need to do is to relax her. It is similar to when you come home after a long day's work, extremely tired, and drop yourself into your recliner. Once you are totally relaxed, you realize that there is a television program playing that you do not like but the remote control is completely across the other side of the room. You are so relaxed that you just allow whatever is on the television to continue to play as it enters your subconscious mind without resistance.

Progressive Relaxation

One of the most common methods a nonanalytical person can use to relax is progressive relaxation. In progressive relaxation, you relax your body one segment at a time, starting with the top of your head and letting go of the stress and tension from every muscle, gradually working all the way down to your feet. After this is done, you may count down starting from the number twenty and continuing backward all the way down to number one, continually using relaxing and calming words throughout the entire process.

 **Question?**

How slow should a nonanalytical session be?
A general rule of thumb is, "You can never go too slow, but you can always go too fast." Progressive relaxation is designed to deeply relax an individual. Think of progressive relaxation as the bore-yourself-silly technique.

The nonanalytical person tends to relax easily and enjoys herself while doing so. Very little induction will be required to hypnotize a nonanalytical person after her second or third session. She can immediately return to how relaxed she was in the previous session in just a few moments.

Devastating Events Can Change Suggestibility

It is interesting to note that someone can change from nonanalytical to analytical in a very short time period. If someone's lifestyle were to change due to some sort of devastating event such as a divorce, a death of a close family member, losing one's job, a near-death experience, or something similar, this could immediately change someone's suggestibility level. If a nonanalytical person suddenly becomes divorced, all of a sudden new responsibilities are thrust onto him, such as possibly working longer hours, absorbing all the family responsibilities, and maybe even being the sole caretaker of children at the same time. This could easily change someone from nonanalytical to analytical. However, if circumstances were to change again for this individual and his scenario was reversed somehow, he could swing all the way back to the nonanalytical side again.

Ten Questions to Determine Your Mindset

This is a test that can be used to determine whether you respond better to analytical or nonanalytical suggestions. People think differently, and they are also hypnotized differently. By answering the following ten questions, you will learn the best type of session to utilize for your self-hypnosis. Read the following questions and write your answers on a separate piece of paper.

1. On your day off, do you prefer relaxing more than keeping busy at home?
2. Do you prefer relaxing at the beach more than catching up on home-improvement projects?
3. When working at home, do you prefer enjoyable music in the background?
4. Do you like to have your favorite refreshment nearby while you are working?
5. While attending a party at a friend's house, do you prefer to sit back and enjoy yourself more than helping out in the kitchen keeping busy?
6. Do you usually enjoy yourself while you work rather than totally concentrating on the job at hand?
7. If you were busy at home and the phone rang, would you answer it immediately even if you have an answering machine?
8. When you have five to six jobs to complete, are you likely to take a short break between them?
9. At the end of your workday, are you more likely to relax rather than find something to do around the house?
10. When making your bed, are you more likely to fluff the pillows and align your belongings in a pleasant manner rather than just getting it done?

Take a moment now to add up your YES and NO responses. If your total includes seven or more YES responses, then you would most likely respond better to a nonanalytical session. If your total includes three or fewer YES responses, then you would most likely respond better to an analytical session in which you would keep your mind busy or distracted while doing something else.

Other Suggestibility Tests

The following two suggestibility tests are alternatives to the ten-question method to determine your level of suggestibility. The best way to conduct these tests is to have someone else read them to you while you use your imagination to follow the instructions. Make sure that the reader takes her time reading the suggestions and pauses wherever she sees the three dots (see the following tests).

Take the time to conduct both of these tests on yourself to decide whether you should use an analytical or nonanalytical session. Both tests should have the same results and will help you to make your decision. Your results from these two tests should also match the results from the ten-question test. If for any reason your results do not match then use the results from these physical suggestibility tests rather than the written one.

The Finger Test

Sit comfortably in your chair and clasp your hands together, interlacing your fingers as if you were praying. Now place your index fingers straight up as if you were making goal posts with your fingers approximately 2 inches apart. Place your hands with your fingers pointing up directly in front of your face approximately 10 inches away. Now concentrate your vision between your two upright fingers, looking nowhere else in the room except between these two fingers. As you are concentrating on the space between your fingers, use your imagination and imagine that a thick rubber band is being placed around your fingertips . . . And you can imagine that rubber band pulling your fingers closer and closer together . . . closer and closer together until they eventually touch . . . and as soon as they touch you can put your hands down . . . (If they have not touched by now continue on with the test.) I'm now placing a second rubber band even thicker than the first one around your fingertips . . . you can feel it pulling your fingers closer and closer together . . . closer and closer until finally they touch.

As a result of the finger test, if your fingers came together and touched fairly easily, then you would be considered nonanalytical. They touched through the power of suggestion. Your strong subconscious mind believed there was a rubber band even though your conscious mind may have been rebelling against it slightly. If your fingers moved very little, however, and did not end up touching, then you are more toward the analytical side. If your fingers did not move at all, that would signify that you are either analytical or you were rebelling against the suggestions. Of course, you are the only one that can really answer that question.

Fact

It is important while conducting these exercises that you let go of any preconceived notions and use your imagination as much as possible. Suggestibility is based on your ability to utilize your imagination. These tests are not a pass or fail situation. If you do not respond to the suggestions, that simply denotes analytical behavior.

The Arm Rising-Falling Test

Once again, have someone else read these instructions to you so that you can use your imagination.

Stand with your feet a comfortable distance apart. Place both of your arms extended straight out in front of you like a zombie. With your right hand, make a thumbs-up gesture. Turn your left hand so that your palm is facing toward the ceiling. Now close your eyes and use your imagination.

Imagine that I am tying the strings attached to twenty-five large helium balloons to your right wrist. As you know, helium is a gas that rises, and you can feel it pulling your right arm upward, light and weightless. Just imagine the colors of the balloons, how large they are, and even the reflections of the light bouncing off of them. Feel them pulling your right arm up, up, up.

Now imagine that on your left palm I am placing the handle connected to a solid steel bucket filled with wet, dirty, muddy water. It is very heavy as you feel it pulling your left arm down, down, down.

The bucket is so very heavy that you can even notice the pain in your upper arm from the weight of holding it.

Your right arm is going up, up, up and your left arm is going down, down, down. Imagine now that I am holding a brick just above the bucket that you are holding in your left hand. In just a moment, on the count of three I am going to drop the brick inside the bucket and it will be very heavy. Ready? One . . . two . . . three! (At the precise moment that you count three, snap your fingers at the same time.)

Now keep your arms right where they are and open your eyes so you can see where your arms are. If your arms had moved in the direction they were suggested, then you would respond best to a nonanalytical session. If your arms did not move at all or very little, then you would respond best to an analytical session.

Chapter 4
Nine Ways to Achieve Self-Hypnosis

There are many different ways to hypnotize yourself, and you have probably done so without even realizing it. It is important to use your imagination as much as possible whenever giving yourself suggestions. Self-hypnosis is based on the use of your imagination. The subconscious mind does not understand the difference between an imagined memory and a real memory. Therefore, according to the mind, whatever you can imagine, combined with your faith and desire, can become reality.

Use Premade CDs or Tapes

Creating your own CDs, tapes, or MP3s is probably the simplest way to conduct self-hypnosis. All you need to do is to record an actual session on a recording device and then sit back comfortably in your favorite chair or recliner and play back the session that you recorded to hypnotize yourself.

 Fact

The word *script* that you will see constantly mentioned throughout this book is a shortened version or slang for the word prescription. It means the same as suggestions. Whatever you tell your subconscious mind, once you have its attention, is your script.

You will find many hypnosis sessions and complete outlines on many different topics in this book that you can record and then listen to. You can also simply create your own suggestions, which you will learn how to do later in this chapter. This is a very convenient way to hypnotize yourself as you can alter your scripts as often as you like depending on the suggestions that you feel you are in need of.

Create Your Own Recorded Sessions

Creating your own home-recorded sessions is a very simple process, and there are many choices available to you. You may choose to record your session on a cassette deck, which you can purchase at most department stores for very little money. Another option is to record a session on a digital recorder, which usually has a better recording quality than a tape recorder. If your computer has a line-in or microphone port, you can record directly to your computer over a microphone.

The advantage of recording your session directly to your computer is that you can then put your session on either a CD or MP3 player. You can then listen to your session as often as you like, take it with you wherever you go, and even put it online so others can listen to it.

 Question?

Can I use my iPod to record or listen to sessions?
For the ultimate in record-and-play simplicity, you can use your iPod for recording and and then listening to your sessions. The iPods made after 2005 (except the Shuffle) have built-in recording capabilities, but you'll need to purchase an add-on mic. Three popular add-on mics are the Belkin TuneTalk Stereo, Griffin iTalk Pro, and the Xtreme Mac MicroMemo. If you want to use your iPod to just listen to sessions, the session must be saved as a WAV, MP3, AAC, or AIFF file before being transferred to your iPod.

Mix, Move, and Edit

Another advantage of recording your session on a computer is that you can use a music-mixing software program, which will allow you to add music or other types of sound effects that you might enjoy to your session. A mixer allows you to overlay various soundtracks that you have created on top of or beside each other. Once you have your voice recorded and downloaded to the mixer, you can then edit as much as you would like.

Many programs allow you to cut or erase outside distractions or mistakes you may have made. Some will allow you to speed up or slow down the speed of the session. You can also adjust the volume on separate tracks, so you can raise your voice or lower the volume of the music to suit your preference. These programs are very easy to use and extremely flexible.

By having your entire session recorded on one of these programs, you will have great flexibility in making future recordings. If you take the time to record each portion or segment of your session, such as the induction, the relaxation portion, and the awakening, on separate tracks, once you decide to make a track for a different session topic, all you will need to record is the actual script or suggestion and simply replace it with the track of the old script from the previous session. Simply insert your suggestions between the relaxation and the awakening portion and your session is finished. This will save you quite a bit of time in the long run.

Computer Programs

There are many programs available on the market today that will do this function for you. Before going down to your local electronics or software store, perform a simple search online to see what is available. You can download some of these recording programs, such as Audacity (*http://audacity.sourceforge.net*), from the Internet for free. In the event that you are not able to find a suitable program, you can visit your local electronics store, where they will have many programs available and in most cases a knowledgeable staff that can help match you to the program that will do what you want.

Alert!

Before running out to purchase all kinds of expensive recording equipment, take a survey of what you may have available to you already. Many digital recorders have adapters that will connect directly to your computer, or you may have a microphone that might also do the job nicely. Try it first then shop if needed.

Some of the programs that are suitable to record in this manner are Audacity, Screenblast Acid, Nero, and Goldwave, just to name a few. Again, your best option is to research programs on your own once you know exactly what it is you would like to do.

Theater of the Mind

The theater of the mind is a wonderful self-hypnosis technique that utilizes imagination training. While sitting in your comfortable, relaxed spot, imagine a movie screen directly in front of you with yourself on it as the main actor. It is important to realize that this technique will work better if you imagine the movie screen outside your head a little ways away from you rather than inside your head.

The Director

You are in complete control of what you the actor perform on the movie screen. What you imagine will immediately take place on the screen. All the controls, props, actors, and background effects are in your mind and are created immediately upon imagining them. As the director, imagine yourself (the actor) having already attained the goal that you would like to achieve.

The subconscious mind imparts the same value to actual and imagined memories. It is important to see yourself as already having accomplished your task. You must see yourself having attained your goal rather than in the process of it. For example, if you are interested in getting a better job, imagine yourself on vacation, spending the money that you received from already having this job, rather than simply being interviewed for the job. If you were to imagine yourself being interviewed for the job, then that is exactly what you will get, an interview for the job.

Creating the Movie

As you create your imagined movie on the movie screen, see yourself as the main actor. It is important that you are the main focus on the screen. To enhance the experience, see everything in as much detail as possible and use emotions, which are very powerful in this process. Imagine the details of what you might wear as the "goal you." What are the details of the scenery around you? Is there anyone else in the picture? If so, what do they look like? Provide details such as their clothing, facial expression, or anything else that makes them stand out.

It's Showtime

In order for the theater of the mind to be most effective, practice it each day for a minimum of twenty-one days without missing a day. Once you begin, if you feel that you have to change anything on your movie screen, do it within the first couple of days. From that point on keep the exact same scene of the movie until the end of the entire twenty-one-day period.

 Essential

You can also record your entire theater of the mind production and listen to it. This is a great way to ensure that you do not change your movie from day to day. You also have the advantage of preplanning it to be sure that it includes details, emotions, and the various senses.

As in any other form of self-hypnosis, find a comfortable place to sit where you will be undisturbed for approximately five to ten minutes and let your movie begin. As you imagine and see yourself as having attained your goal, see the details and feel as many emotions as possible about having attained your goal. Include as many of the five senses as possible in your scenario. Are you able to smell, taste, hear, see, or feel anything?

It is extremely important while you are conducting this exercise that the goal you have chosen is one that you feel is attainable. You must be able to see yourself accomplishing this task. If you find it is not believable, then you may want to alter your imagination scenario to one that you feel can be accomplished. Once you have accomplished the task, you can always raise or increase your limits at that time.

Theater of the Mind Script

Close your eyes and relax . . . Take a deep breath . . . exhale . . . and take a second deep breath . . . and exhale, and on your third deep breath, hold it for about three seconds . . . and exhale and relax.

I would like you to use your imagination right now. Imagine, or just think about, yourself sitting comfortably in front of a large movie screen and imagine that you are seeing a motion picture of yourself. See it as vividly and in as much detail as possible. See yourself in this motion picture reacting successfully, in the ideal situation, having already attained your goal. As you are visualizing yourself as this successful person . . . see yourself as the main actor or lead person on your screen . . . How do you feel now that you have become the person that you would like to be . . . (pause) . . . Feel the emotions . . . What are you feeling? . . . Maybe confidence . . . pride . . . fulfillment . . . satisfaction . . . relief . . . happiness . . . (pause) . . . What emotions are you feeling exactly . . . Let those emotions fill you up . . . (pause) . . . Let them grow within you . . . (pause) . . . What are you hearing associated with your new goal? What are others saying about you? How do they feel about your accomplishments? . . . (pause) . . . I'd also like you to visualize and feel what you think is different

. . . What is different now that you have attained your goal? How is your life changed? . . . (pause) . . . Are you enjoying any more freedoms associated with this attainment? . . . Think about them, get them clearly in your mind as you visualize yourself standing in front of you on that motion picture screen . . . (pause) . . . See the details . . . What are you wearing? . . . What are you doing? . . . What else do you notice that is associated with this now orderly achievement? . . . (pause) . . . Remember the imagining of yourself doing something with enough detail is equal to the actual experience as far as your subconscious mind is concerned. So see yourself for just a few more moments having achieved your new habit . . . (pause) . . .

You are in control of your life now . . . You have created and attained a new positive habit . . . With the power of your subconscious mind, it is very easy to do . . . You have allowed the past disorder to fade away like an unwanted memory . . . and now you move forward . . . The disorder of the past has been replaced with order. The dysfunctionality replaced with functionality. So once again feel that wonderful sense of satisfaction and achievement. It is coming from that strong subconscious mind that you have. You have created your goal and through these daily exercises are maintaining it, creating a permanent habit of change.

At the count of three you will come all the way back to the here and now . . .

One . . . Beginning to come all the way back.

Two . . . Feeling totally relaxed and comfortable.

Three . . . Eyes wide open and feeling great.

Six-Step Visualization Process

With this form of self-hypnosis, you create your own simple script that includes the following six criteria. Once you have created your script, sit in your comfortable place that you use for hypnosis, close your eyes, and take three deep breaths. Once your eyes are closed and you are relaxed, recite your script over and over. Prepare your script so that it will be easy for you to visualize or imagine it. As you recite your script, you may find that you skip or forget some of the words. That is not a problem as long as you are using your imagination and seeing yourself accomplishing the task that is on your script. Replay the scene over and over in your mind for approximately three to five minutes, after which time you will come out of hypnosis by counting to three and opening your eyes.

Following are the six criteria you need to create your self-hypnosis script. Take a few moments to study each one as they are very important to your overall success.

Simple

Create a script that is very simple so it is easy to remember once in hypnosis. Writing one sentence is good, and two sentences are adequate; however, three sentences are too many. When writing your script, think whether it would be too much for a four-year-old child to remember. This will help you to keep it simple.

Believable

To make a script that is successful, make sure that the goal you have in mind is attainable. Do you believe that you can attain this goal? If you are going to hypnotize yourself to be able to run a marathon but you have difficulty running to your mailbox, then your suggestions would not be believable. You may want to make suggestions for running back and forth to your mailbox a few times, and once you have attained that goal increase it in small increments to build up to running a marathon.

 Fact

Here's a famous bit of wisdom: How do you eat an elephant? One bite at a time! If you try to eat an elephant all at once, you will find that it is unattainable. You will choke on it. It is beyond your reach. You have to take it in increments and eventually you can finish it.

Keep in mind, however, that if you break down your goal into smaller increments, once you have attained the downsized goal you could reach a mental plateau. This means that once you attain the goal that you set forth, your mind will remain there until it is given a new goal. Therefore, you will have to remember to change the goal to a new plateau. In the case of the marathon, you may want to increase it to a half mile. Once you attain that goal, then increase it to a mile.

This is especially true in the area of weight loss. For example, say someone wants to lose 200 pounds; that is an extremely large goal that may be unattainable. However, if the goal is broken down to twenty pounds at a time, once you lose the first twenty pounds, you may find that you will remain at that weight until the plateau is removed and a suggestion for another twenty pounds is inserted in its place.

Measurable

Whatever goal you want to accomplish, be specific as to how you are going to do it. It must be measurable. The more detail that you put into a suggestion, the more attainable it will be. If your goal is something that can be measured by ounces, pounds, time periods, repetitions, or days, break it down to those specific measurements.

For example, "I want to walk on my treadmill every day" is not a measurable goal. Exactly what day of the week and how far are you going to walk? You may want to walk every weekday. Then how far are you going to walk each day? If you simply say "I am going to walk on my treadmill every day," then by simply turning it on and walking three steps will satisfy your subconscious mind that it has attained your goal. Are you going to walk one mile, two miles, more? You must be specific. What time of the day are you going to walk? If you simply say "When I get up in the morning," that will not be sufficient because if you are late for work you will not take the time to walk. Be specific with what time you will begin. Putting it all together, you may want to say something like, "Every weekday at 6 A.M. I am walking two miles on my treadmill." That suggestion is now measurable.

Remember that the subconscious mind is like a four-year-old child, and, like a child, it will take the path of least resistance. If you leave an easy way out so that you do not have to exercise, your mind will take that path. Also remember that the conscious mind, being a creature of habit, fights against change. Therefore, taking additional time to exercise each day may be difficult at first due to your natural resistance.

Positive

Any suggestion that you create, whether for exercise or another type of script, should always be positive. Never create a negative suggestion. Scare tactics or other negative statements, such as "cigarettes taste like rotten cabbage," have no place in positive conditioning.

In addition to creating all of your suggestions in a positive manner, try to make them overly positive. Rather than saying a statement like, "every day I am exercising . . . ," change that statement to, "every day I am excited to exercise . . . " With overly positive statements you will notice a great difference in both your desire to accomplish your task as well as your success.

Present Tense

Your suggestions should always be in the present tense. For example, "I am drinking water." By making the statement in the present tense you can actually visualize yourself in the action. Present tense statements carry action with them. If you make a statement in the past tense ("I have been drinking water"), then your mind will feel that you have accomplished the task and has nothing left to do. If you say, "I will be drinking water," then your mind will say, "Okay I'll just wait." Using the present tense will greatly aid you in imagining and visualizing your goal.

Carry a Reward

Every statement should carry a reward with it, something you can give yourself once you have accomplished the task. Remember that the subconscious mind is like a four-year-old child. If you were to confront a four-year-old and tell him to pick up all his toys in his room, chances are you would not have much success. However, if you were to tell the same child if he picked up all the toys in his room you would give him a bowl of ice cream, chances are that the room would be cleaned up very quickly. Your subconscious mind works the same way. If you give yourself a reward, you will be much more likely to work toward your goal.

Alert!

Your reward should be appropriate to your goal. For example, if you want to lose twenty pounds, you may not want to reward yourself with a Twinkie every weekend. A good reward would be to buy yourself a new suit, dress, scarf, or even a pair of shoes.

In many cases the goal itself is reward enough. For example, "Every weekday at three o'clock I am walking from my house to the high school and back and feeling healthy, happy, and strong." In this scenario, the "healthy, happy, and strong" are the goals.

Here is another example of a completed suggestion following all six criteria. "Every day before lunch and dinner I am drinking a sixteen-ounce glass of water, which helps me to eat less, and I feel great."

Autosuggestion Script

Autosuggestion is simply the art of giving yourself positive affirmations or suggestions. This can easily be done by creating a self-affirmation or autosuggestion script, recording it on your choice of recording device, and then playing it back to yourself.

The most successful way of using an autosuggestion script is to repeat what is being said on the recording back to yourself either quietly or out loud. In order to be able to do that, when you are recording your autosuggestion script you must give yourself a break or pause between sentences so you will have time to repeat the suggestion to yourself.

 Essential

When you repeat the suggestions back to yourself, it is important to not only say the words but to use your imagination and visualize or imagine the suggestions taking place as well as involve as many feelings and pictures as possible.

Following is an autosuggestion script that you may use. Read the entire script onto a tape recorder. Play it back while relaxing somewhere comfortable. Repeat the words to yourself quietly or out loud, whichever you prefer. You could also have someone recite the page to you slowly while you repeat the words quietly back to yourself.

How It Works

Where you see the words "insert your script here" is where you would insert whatever script you desire. Wherever you see the three consecutive dots, be sure to take time to pause. The dots are where you would take the time to repeat the script to yourself. Where you see more than three dots, pause a little longer.

Autosuggestion Script

I feel rested . . . I feel safe . . . I feel relaxed . . . I am rested . . . I am safe . . . I am relaxed . . . I feel calm . . . I feel secure . . . I am open-minded . . . And as I open my mind . . . all the muscles in my body begin to relax . . . every muscle, beginning from the top of my head . . . relaxes . . . and lets go of its hold . . . . . . Moving down through my body . . . Just letting go completely . . . all the way down to the bottom of my feet . . . I feel rested . . . I feel open . . . I feel relaxed . . .

And as I breathe in deeply . . . and exhale slowly . . . I let go of all the tension . . . and the anxiety . . . in my body . . . leaving me rested . . . and calm . . . I feel rested . . . I feel open . . . I feel relaxed . . . My mind is now totally open and accepting . . . of the suggestions I am about to give myself . . .

(Insert your script here.)

I feel rested . . . I feel safe . . . I feel relaxed . . . I am rested . . . I am safe . . . I am relaxed . . .

In a moment you will open your eyes feeling wonderful in every way . . .

One . . . feeling better than before . . .

Two . . . eyes beginning to open . . . and

Three . . . eyes wide open, feeling wonderful in every way.

Read Your Way to Success

Reading is very hypnotic. Think back to when you were a child and your parents read fairy tales to you or maybe even a time where you read fairy tales or similar children's stories to your own children. As you remember these stories that were read to you, vivid pictures came to mind of the characters and the situations that they found themselves in. While you were reading or hearing the stories, your imagination brought the characters to life in the story. The reason you were able to imagine them that way is that you were open to suggestion, which is also known as being in hypnosis.

Therefore, any time you read suggestions or affirmations to yourself or even to someone else and you are open to suggestion, you are hypnotizing yourself. It will be even more effective if you allow your imagination to run free and create the story or suggestions in your mind. The more vivid and full of feeling you can make the experience, the more effective it will be to you.

This is one of the many ways you can utilize the upcoming sessions included in this book. You can either read them onto a recording device so you can play it back to hypnotize yourself, or you can simply relax somewhere and read them on the page.

Writing Is Hypnotic

There is something magical that happens when you write things down. The act of writing ingrains things in your subconscious mind. By writing things down, you remember them more and you are more aware of what you are doing. In fact, many weight-loss programs have you write down all of the foods you eat on a daily basis as a means of helping you to eat the proper items.

In marital or relationship counseling, partners are often asked to make a list of their favorite qualities about each other. By making this list they learn more about what they like about their partner. It helps them to see the good features in their partner that they may have overlooked before their initial problems. It often helps them see what they initially saw in their partner that drew them toward each other.

Take the time to write a script for yourself. To make it even more effective, write it in a letter to yourself about what you would like to see yourself accomplish. Be as detailed as possible and write it in a way that you can use your imagination to visualize your goal effectively. If you like, you can even address it to yourself and mail it.

ⓔ Question?

What is the purpose of writing down your goals?
If you have not written your goals, then they are probably too vague and therefore not yet unattainable. Writing your goals in detail helps you break down exactly what they are. There is an added visual element as well, which enhances the process.

Daydreaming: Not Just a Pastime

Daydreaming occurs in the theta brain wave state. This is the state your mind is in just before you fall asleep. You can frequently see young people daydreaming as they sit in class. Especially during boring lectures, students daydream about being home, having fun, or maybe even off having an exciting adventure.

Daydreaming is an effective form of self-hypnosis as well as a wonderful way to program your mind to attain your goals. Find the time to relax sometime during your day and simply close your eyes and allow your mind to roam free. Allow yourself to think about obtaining your goal and just let your mind roam, focusing on the same topic. You may even want to ask yourself questions pertaining to your goal and let your mind show you the end result of what you are seeking. For instance, if your goal is being an expert public speaker, allow your mind to roam free and see yourself onstage dressed professionally, walking back and forth energetically while speaking to a group of people. Allow your mind to create the audience looking very enthusiastic and applauding frequently throughout your presentation. See yourself surrounded by impressed audience members after the presentation asking for your autograph.

Create Your Own Subliminals

Subliminals are another form of self-hypnosis that you can listen to any time during the day, no matter what you are doing. Subliminals are suggestions that are often masked by music or other distractions. The concept is that if you are not listening to the suggestions consciously, you will not fight them. Since you are listening to other distractions, such as music, noises, binary beats, or even other voices, you are not hearing the suggestions directly but are receiving them subconsciously. This way the suggestions enter directly into your subconscious mind without hindrance. This is like doing your homework while there is a television program playing in the background. Although you are focusing on your task at hand, everything that is being played on the television is going right into your subconscious mind without being challenged. Your conscious mind can only do so many things at once and therefore allows the background stimuli to enter.

To make your own subliminals, record your entire session onto your computer mixing device or someplace where you can add several tracks to it. Normally when you make your MP3s or CDs on your computer you would mix your track of background music softly in the background so you can hear the voice giving the suggestions over the music. When making a subliminal, however, you raise the background music to mask your voice so that the words cannot be easily heard. You may even want to insert background noises such as drums or even the sound of a metronome.

 Fact

When creating your subliminal CDs or MP3s, be sure not to use any phrases having to do with being sleeping or deep relaxation. This way the suggestions can be listened to throughout your entire day as background sound whether you are working, watching television, cooking, or even driving a car.

Another way to make subliminals is to record your session; however, rather than adding a track of music to mask it, record several other vocal sessions playing simultaneously with yours. It should sound like being in a room full of people with five conversations going on at once. If you listen to one conversation in the room you will be able to focus on that one conversation; however, the other four conversations tend to blend into each other and are shut out by the conscious mind. Since the subconscious mind can do unlimited tasks simultaneously, it receives the suggestions from the other four conversations without hindrance. So by giving five scripts simultaneously, the conscious mind cannot rebel against all of them and most of the suggestions will reach the subconscious mind.

The advantage of this is you can make five sessions that are exactly the same, only stagger them slightly on your mixing board so that they sound garbled when played together, or you can actually make five completely different sessions so there will be no chance your conscious mind can follow them. Although making subliminals with five or more different voices may be more effective than conventional subliminals with music, you will find the ones with relaxing music, waterfalls, and nature sounds to be much more enjoyable.

Chapter 5
Getting the Ball Rolling

In Chapter 3 you learned how to test your suggestibility to find out whether you are analytical or not. Now with the results of those tests in mind you will learn how to determine which is the best type of session for you to achieve optimum results so that you may begin the self-help process. Although one session may be more effective for you, you may want to try both to see the differences.

Analytical Versus Nonanalytical

While anyone of reasonable intelligence can be hypnotized, not everyone is hypnotized in the same manner. Although relaxation is the way that most people are hypnotized, not everyone is able to relax easily; therefore, different options are available for those people. Sessions must be tailored to the individual.

Results of Testing

As previously mentioned, there are two major categories that people fall within: analytical or nonanalytical. Use the suggestibility tests in Chapter 3 to find which category best suits you. Very rarely will you find someone who is either 100 percent analytical or 100 percent nonanalytical. Most likely you'll find yourself somewhere on this scale between the two endpoints.

Analytical _____ | _____ **Nonanalytical**

On the suggestibility tests, if you followed the instructions and responded quickly and easily you would be placed on the nonanalytical side. The quicker that you responded to the suggestions, the more to the right side you would be. If you reacted slower to the suggestions, you would be placed more toward the center according to how slow or little you reacted. If you did not react to the suggestions or reacted very little, you would be placed on the analytical or left side of the center. If you reacted very little you would be placed more to the center, and if you did not react at all you would be more toward the left.

Take a few moments now to look at your results from the tests in Chapter 3 and place yourself on the scale according to your results. Now that you have found where you rank on the scale, the next step is in knowing how to decipher the information. Depending on which side of the scale you ended up on, this would tell you whether you need to use an analytical or nonanalytical approach. For a nonanalytical session, the more common type of relaxation session is all you will need. If you are on the analytical side, you will have to use an approach that will keep your mind busy.

 Essential

Even though 80 percent of society is nonanalytical and only 20 percent is analytical, keep in mind that the analytical session works on anyone while the nonanalytical session may not. The reason for this is that not everyone can be relaxed; however, anyone can be kept busy.

Preparation for Self-Hypnosis

There are a few simple procedures that must be followed in preparation for your session to begin. Find a quiet, out-of-the-way location where you will not be disturbed. Ensure you will not be interrupted by telephones, beepers, radios, or anything else that may distract you.

Make sure all pets are out of the room as they may also disturb you during the session.

For safety reasons, it is important that you do not to listen to or participate in hypnosis sessions while driving a motor vehicle or operating any type of dangerous equipment. If you are simply listening to sub-liminal suggestions or affirmations while working, driving, or operating any type of dangerous equipment, be sure that they do not include the words *sleep* or *deep relaxation*.

Take a moment to get yourself comfortable in a chair, recliner, or couch, ensuring that your neck and head are supported. Be sure not to cross your arms or legs during the session as your body posture should be free-flowing and relaxed. It is better to place your arms either on the arms of your chair or on your lap.

Analytical Induction Process and Template

You are now ready to begin your session. Take a moment to decide exactly which of the nine procedures you are going to use as described in Chapter 4. The upcoming hypnosis session templates can be used in many differ-ent ways, or you may want to even create your own session, which will be discussed later in this chapter. You need to decide what it is you would like to be hypnotized for, choose the desired scripts, and insert your goal in the template where it says "insert your script here."

Instructions

One of the ways you can use a hypnotic template is to find a comfortable, quiet place where you can relax and simply read the session to yourself. Remember, the key ingredient when reading the session to yourself is to use your imagination.

 Fact

When reciting the template to yourself or on a recording device, it is important to read very slowly and pause for a moment whenever you see the three consecutive dots. If you recite the session too quickly, you may find it frustrating when you take time to listen to it.

You can record the template, then find a comfortable place where you can sit back, play the session, and listen to it. You may have your eyes open or closed; however, the session will be much more successful with your eyes closed. You can also have someone else read it to you while you are sitting comfortably with your eyes closed.

Template #1: Cities of the Alphabet

Close your eyes . . . take a deep breath, hold it for a moment and exhale . . . take a second deep breath, as deep as you can, hold it for a moment and exhale . . . and on your third deep breath hold it for about three seconds . . . and exhale and relax . . . with each breath that you take from this point forward, allow yourself to relax deeper and deeper . . .

What I would like for you to do now, with your eyes closed, is to imagine that right in front of you, within your arm's reach, is a very large full-size map on the wall . . . so close to you that if you were to reach out, you could draw on it . . . See it in your mind's eye . . . Now imagine this map is of the United States, or whatever country you are familiar with, and that the names of the cities are left blank . . . It is a map that you will use to find the cities and write their names on . . . Look to your right and you'll find a small table just beside you, and a colored pencil set is right there on the table . . . There are twenty-six colored pencils on it . . . Visually scan the map from left to right . . . and scan back from right to left . . . Now maybe you see the map pretty clearly in your mind's eye . . . And maybe you don't . . . either way, just imagine you can see it . . . Now scan the map with your eyes and find any city on the map that begins with the letter A . . . Point it out on the map with one of the colored pencils . . . any color pencil you like . . . and write the city's name down on the top of the point where the city is with the colored pencil you chose . . . Scan the map again to find the second city, one that begins with a letter B . . . Point it out with a different colored pencil and write its name on the top of the point with the colored pencil you chose.

Just hold it a moment and wait for my further instructions . . . When I tell you to go ahead, you will continue to search for a city that begins with the letter C . . . and write the name down with a new colored pencil just like you did with the letter A and B before . . . Then search for a city that begins with the letter D . . . and write the name down and so forth . . . Remember, you should use as many different colors as you can when writing the city names on the map . . . Once you begin your task . . . from that point forward . . . don't listen to me anymore . . . By that I mean, don't make any effort to listen to me. I will be speaking, of course, and you will be hearing me, but don't try to follow my instructions or what I am saying, because I will be speaking directly to your subconscious mind, which always hears and always pays attention . . . Your job is to keep going, finding each city on the map, going through the alphabet . . . finding and writing each city with a different color pencil in succession . . . paying no attention to me at all . . . until you have finished the whole job . . . then you can just relax and listen to me again. By that time, you will be in a deep relaxed state . . . Remember, when I tell you to go ahead . . . you'll continue going through the alphabet, paying no further attention to me until you have found and written each city's name and have gotten all the way to the letter Z.

Now it's time to begin . . . so scan the map and find a city beginning with the letter C . . . and keep on going, but paying no further attention to me . . . Just find the city and write its name down . . . find another one and write that one down . . . on and on in succession through the alphabet . . . taking your time . . . Each city you find and each city you write down causes you to relax more and more . . . Each city you find and each city you write causes you to drift more easily and more readily into hypnosis . . . The closer you come to the letter Z, the deeper into hypnosis you go . . . With each city you find and each city you write down, you drift down and down, deeper and deeper into the hypnotic state . . .

(Insert your script here.)

In just a moment I will count to five, and at the count of five you will open your eyes feeing wonderful and refreshed . . .

One . . . You are starting to emerge from hypnosis

Two . . . Feeling so wonderful

Three . . . Your mind is clear and alert

Four . . . Your eyes are starting to open . . . and

Five . . . Eyes wide open and feeling fine.

 Question?

> **What if client has finished the exercise before I finish reading the script?**
> It doesn't matter whether you finish or not. If she has finished the exercise she can simply relax and listen to the remainder of the session. If she is not finished then she will simply open her eyes once the awakening has been recited.

Template #2: Writing in the Sand

Close your eyes and take a slow, deep breath . . . take another slow, deep breath . . . and with your third deep breath inhale slowly, holding your breath for at least three seconds . . . now exhale, allowing all of your stress and worry to leave you as the air passes out of your chest . . . feeling more relaxed as the air passes your lips . . . all stress and worry leaving your body as you become more and more relaxed . . . pay attention to your breathing . . . with each breath you are becoming more calm and relaxed . . . now use your imagination to see a beautiful walking trail with large trees lining both sides of the path . . . as you walk down the path notice the sound of the birds . . . the light and fluffy clouds in the bright blue sky above . . . as you walk down the path you notice a beach off in the distance . . . as you walk closer to the beach you feel yourself becoming more and more relaxed . . . you come up to the beach and walk down toward the water. You notice that the sand is very smooth and fine . . . as you are looking out at the ocean you can feel the waves covering your feet and then washing out once again. The water is very warm and relaxing. You begin to pay close attention to this washing in and out motion of the waves. You notice that one of the incoming waves brought with it a long piece of driftwood that you pick up. It is about three feet long. With the wood you draw a circle in the sand . . . and within a few moments you notice how the new wave coming in washes away the circle that you just drew and then goes back out to the ocean. It is as if you had a clean slate to write on once again. You then decide to draw a large number twenty-five in the sand. Use your imagination and do that now . . . now imagine a wave coming back in, covering your number and washing it out . . . now draw a large number twenty-four in the sand . . . taking your time to draw as neatly as possible . . . and wait for the next wave to wash it away . . . and draw the number twenty-three in the sand . . . and once again watch the wave come in and wash the number away, leaving your drawing area clean.

In just a moment you will continue drawing the numbers in the sand, taking your time and waiting for each wave to come in and wash your numbers away. Starting with your next number, which is twenty-two, going all the way down to the number one. Once you begin the task, do not pay attention to my voice anymore; do not try to follow my instructions. You will be hearing me, of course, but I will be speaking to your subconscious mind, which always pays attention. Your job will be to continue drawing each number, focusing on what you are doing and watching the numbers as they wash away until you get all the way to the number one. Once you have drawn the number one and it washes away, you can then relax and listen to me once again.

Go ahead and begin now by drawing the number twenty-two in the sand with your stick . . . and watch as the waves come in and wash it away . . . paying no further attention to me now . . . just drawing the number and watching it get washed away . . . and the next one . . . as you continue until you are finished with your task . . . with each number you draw and each number that washes away you are becoming more peaceful and relaxed . . . with each number you draw you are becoming more open to suggestion . . . the closer you come to the number one . . . the deeper into relaxation you go . . .

(Insert your script here.)

In just a moment I will count to five, and at the count of five you will open your eyes feeing wonderful and refreshed . . .

One . . . You are starting to emerge from hypnosis

Two . . . Feeling so wonderful

Three . . . Your mind is clear and alert

Four . . . Your eyes are starting to open . . . and

Five . . . Eyes wide open and feeling fine.

Nonanalytical Induction Process and Template

The nonanalytical template can be used in the same way as the analytical session. When reading the nonanalytical session, recite it very slowly. The key to a nonanalytical session (in addition to using your imagination) is to relax.

Template #1: Gradual, Downward Relaxation

Close your eyes . . . take a deep breath . . . take a second deep breath, as deep as you can . . . and on your third deep breath hold it for about three seconds . . . and exhale and relax . . . with each breath that you take, allow yourself to relax deeper and deeper . . .

I'm going to have you relax each part of your body, starting from the top of your head going all the way down to the bottom of your feet . . . and as I mention each part, just allow everything to let go . . . starting with the top of your head . . . your scalp and your forehead . . . let go of all the tension and stress . . . your eyebrows . . . your eyelids . . . feel that relaxation going down through your cheeks and your nose . . . relax all the muscles around your mouth and lips . . . relax your chin and jaw . . . and allow all those muscles in your face to just relax and let go . . . feel that relaxation going down into your neck and shoulders . . . get rid of any tension that might be in your shoulder area . . . it should feel good to do that . . . relax your arms . . . all the way down to your hands and fingertips . . . just let go . . .

let go completely . . . and notice how deep your breathing has become . . . so much more relaxed than just a few moments ago . . . and as you breathe in deeply and exhale slowly . . . allow all the muscles in your chest to just relax . . . all the way down to your stomach, get rid of any tension that might be in your stomach area . . . down to your hips . . . just let go completely . . . and your legs relax . . . your thighs . . . your knees . . . relax your calves and your ankles . . . feel that relaxation going down into your feet . . . and even your toes just relax completely . . . as you drift down deeper into a very relaxed state . . .

In just a moment I'm going to count from twenty down to one . . . And as I say each number, I'd like you to imagine the number, think about it, and quietly spell the number to yourself, which will help you to deepen your own relaxation allowing you to relax at your own pace.

So let's begin with 20 as you spell it . . . t-w-e-n-t-y . . . 19 . . . n-i-n-e-t-e-e-n . . . 18 . . . all the way down deep . . . 17 . . . 16 . . . deeper and deeper . . . 15 . . . keep on spelling the numbers to yourself quietly . . . 14 . . . just let yourself go . . . 13 . . . 12 . . . give yourself the permission that this is what you want to do . . . 11 . . . 10 . . . allow yourself to just let go . . . 9 . . . 8 . . . deeper and deeper . . . 7 . . . 6 . . . all the way down deep . . . 5 . . . 4 . . . tired and drowsy . . . 3 . . . 2 . . . so very relaxed . . . and finally . . . 1 . . . deep . . . deep . . . relaxation.

(Insert your script here.)

In just a moment I will count to five, and at the count of five you will open your eyes feeing wonderful and refreshed . . .

One . . . You are starting to emerge from hypnosis

Two . . . Feeling so wonderful

Three . . . Your mind is clear and alert

Four . . . Your eyes are starting to open . . . and

Five . . . Eyes wide open and feeling fine.

Fact

A good technique to use to ensure that you are pausing long enough between each number is to take a deep breath before moving on. Even though it may seem like an extremely long time, you will realize once you are listening to it in a hypnotic state that it is not. You may even want to go back and record it even slower the next time.

Template #2: Breathing Relaxation

Close your eyes . . . take a deep breath . . . take a second deep breath, as deep as you can . . . and on your third deep breath hold it for about three seconds . . . and exhale and relax . . . with each breath that you take, allow yourself to relax deeper and deeper . . .

Now I'd like you to imagine yourself resting comfortably in your chair . . . that's right . . . just allow the chair to support you, settling down easily, with your arms resting at your sides or gently on your lap; head and neck in a comfortable upright position . . . Very good . . . and now that you are very comfortable, I'd like you to become aware of your breathing . . . Feel the coolness of your breath as it enters your nostrils, noticing your chest as it rises and falls . . . rises and falls, in an easy and natural rhythm . . . your own perfect and natural rhythm . . . just breathing in . . . and out . . . in . . . and out . . . Just allow your awareness to focus on your breath . . . Just allow your awareness to remain focused on your breath as you allow it to quiet and deepen your relaxation . . . deeper and deeper . . . and begin to notice that, as you allow yourself to become more and more relaxed, it is easy and natural . . . You do not need to make any conscious effort to breathe. Your marvelous subconscious mind is taking care of your breathing, from the moment of your birth throughout your life, for as long as you live . . . And just as your subconscious mind is the guardian of your breath and all your bodily functions, it is also the creator of your dreams and the champion of your highest aspirations . . . always supporting you, protecting you, and working for your greatest good . . . Knowing this, you can relax even more deeply with each and every breath that you take . . . from this point onward you can allow yourself to simply rest as you breathe . . . rest and relax . . . rest and relax . . . deeper and deeper . . . knowing that the more you relax, the deeper you go, and the deeper you go, the more you can relax, allowing your subconscious mind, with all its awesome power, to work on your behalf, to easily and effortlessly understand and receive every positive suggestion, and allow it to become a part of you for as long as it is of use to you . . .

(Insert your script here.)

In just a moment I will count to five, and at the count of five you will open your eyes feeing wonderful and refreshed . . .

One . . . You are starting to emerge from hypnosis

Two . . . Feeling so wonderful

Three . . . Your mind is clear and alert

Four . . . Your eyes are starting to open . . . and

Five . . . Eyes wide open and feeling fine.

Creating Your Own Sessions

Once you understand the basics of self-hypnosis you may want to create your own sessions. Here is a format that you can use to easily build your own sessions from scratch. Also included are the instructions on how to create your own scripts.

Induction

The first step of your own hypnosis script is the induction. The induction is what you say to initially help yourself settle down and relax. Most people use what is known as a body scan. The body scan is simply naming each part or segment of your body, from head to toe or even from toe to head, relaxing each part as you mention it. If you desire, you can be creative while mentioning each part of the body by moving it slightly or whatever you would like as a way of helping you to focus more on that specific muscle group.

Deepener or Vehicle

After the induction or body scan comes what is known as a deepener or a vehicle. The deepener is used primarily for the nonanalytical subject as it is designed to help the subject to relax more and bring him to a deeper state. The vehicle is used for the analytical subject and is the tool designed to keep his mind busy while the suggestions are being read so as to bypass the rebellious conscious mind.

In creating a nonanalytical deepener, you have an unlimited variety of choices available. One deepener is to simply count down from a certain number, such as twenty, counting backward slowly all the way to the number one to allow you time to relax. You can involve more visual things within your counting, such as counting steps while walking down them. You can also count the floors on an elevator as you descend. If you do not wish to count, you can just create relaxing scenes such as lying on a hammock in the middle of a field of wildflowers or relaxing on a mountainside while watching the sunset. Anything that helps you relax will work just fine.

Ⓔ Alert!

When creating an analytical vehicle, do not make the task too difficult. Although the idea is to keep your mind busy, if the task is too difficult, such as complex math or other similar forms of mental multitasking, you may get frustrated and stop doing the task. If this happens, you may be even more resistant to the suggestions due to frustration.

The vehicle, also known as the analytical vehicle, is simply a technique designed to keep the subject's mind busy. The vehicle can be any simple task, from drawing numbers or letters in succession on a blackboard to lying on the ground while watching clouds form into descending numbers. It's similar to the example of trying to do your taxes and have a conversation at the same time. You must let go of the conversation to do a good job on your taxes.

Creating Your Own Suggestions/Script

There are many scripts in this book that you may use in your sessions. As you become comfortable with using them you will eventually begin to create your own suggestions targeting more precise issues.

 Fact

Keep in mind that in hypnosis you are speaking to the subconscious mind, which is similar to a four-year-old child. Creating a script is as simple as deciding what you would tell a four-year-old child to do in order to change.

A script can be as long or as short as you like, but it should be long enough to get the point across. You can write a script for any area that you can improve in. Before writing a script, take the time to break down your topic into as many separate aspects or areas that you can in order to cover it properly.

Topic_____

Idea_____

Aspect #1_____

Aspect #2_____

Aspect #3_____

Aspect #4_____

Aspect #5_____

Once you fill in the various aspects of the topic, place them in the chronological order that seems to make the most sense.

Topic Order

#1_____

#2_____

#3_____

#4_____

#5_____

Once you have done this, take each aspect and turn it into a paragraph. Following are some additional items to help your script:

- When writing your script, try to include as many of the five senses as possible: sight, hearing, touch, smell, taste.
- Always use positive, active wording (for example, *excited*, *energized*, *anxious*, *happily*, and so on).
- Make all suggestions believable.
- Include confidence, self-esteem, and relaxation statements.
- Use pictures and imaginative phrases. The subconscious mind reacts better to pictures rather than just words. Use your imagination as much as possible, seeing the end result as having already been attained rather than the progression of reaching it.
- Include emotions. Whatever emotions or feelings can be associated with the subject will help the script be more effective.

Now put it all together and write your script.

Awakening

The awakening is a simple procedure where you simply count forward three to five numbers and then open your eyes. The reason for a proper awakening is so you can emerge from hypnosis gradually in a relaxed state. It is not vital to have an awakening as you may just open your eyes on your own; however, inserting an awakening gives a session a formal ending.

Imagination Training Equals Real Results

Using your imagination is the key for successful results. The subconscious mind does not understand the difference between an imagined memory and a real memory. For example, imagine your favorite dessert prepared perfectly in every way and served to you on a silver platter. You may find while imagining this treat your mind begins to respond in similar ways to how it would if the dessert were actually in front of you. Your mouth may begin to water and you may begin to get hungry. Once you have done this exercise, if you close your eyes a week from now and imagine your dessert once again, this same picture of your dessert on a silver platter would come back to you as if it were an actual memory rather than an imagined one.

 Essential

You may have seen this concept of imagining things into reality with people who tend to overexaggerate. People who overexaggerate stories that happened to them often begin to believe the exaggerations to the point that they become a reality for that person.

The more detail you can put in your imagination, the more real results become. When using your imagination, involve as many as your senses as possible. For example, if you are imagining food, what does it taste or smell like? If you are imagining a coffee table, what color is it and what does the texture of the wood feel like?

Follow Up for Success

It is important to realize that habits are replaced rather than eliminated. The habits that you presently have and would like to change have been created by you repeatedly doing them over and over. Habits do not happen overnight. In order to replace your habit, a new one must be created, which also will not happen overnight. In order to create a permanent habit, suggestions must be given repeatedly over a period of time until the new behavior is accepted and becomes a permanent part of you.

A Follow-up Session

This follow-up session can be listened to each day from day two onward, regardless of what the topic is you are being hypnotized for. It is a generic follow-up session that can be used for any topic. It guides you through utilizing your imagination to create a new habit.

This program will work just as successfully whether you go into a deep hypnosis, a light hypnosis, or if you don't even go into hypnosis at all. The main purpose of the sessions is to use your imagination as a means to create new memories, because the subconscious mind cannot differentiate between an imagined memory or an actual memory. Therefore, whether you go into hypnosis to visualize the scenes or simply listen to the instructions and let your imagination go, the same purpose is accomplished.

Alert!

In the theater of the mind portion of the follow-up session, you will be asked to imagine yourself on a movie screen directly in front of you as already having attained your goal. Once you have created this movie, it is important that you use the *same image* each day without changing it until you have attained your goal.

Close your eyes and relax. Take a deep breath . . . and exhale . . . and take a second deep breath . . . and exhale . . . and on your third deep breath, hold it for about three seconds . . . and exhale and relax.

I'm going to have you relax every part of your body, starting with the top of your head . . . your scalp and your forehead . . . your eyebrows and your eyelids . . . and feel that relaxation going down through your cheeks and your nose . . . relax your mouth and lips . . . make sure your teeth are not clenched together . . . and just relax . . . relax your chin and your jaw . . . and allow all of those muscles in your face to just let go . . . and your neck relaxes . . . all the way down to your shoulders . . . get rid of any tension that might be in your shoulder area . . . and your arms relax . . . your upper arms . . . your elbows . . . relax your wrists . . . your hands . . . even the fingers relax . . . and notice how deep and regular your breathing has become . . .

feel your breathing . . . notice the contraction and expansion of your diaphragm and your chest . . . and allow your chest muscles to relax completely . . . down to your stomach . . . feel your stomach muscles relax and let go . . . get rid of any tension that might be in that area . . . just allow everything to let go completely . . . and your hips relax . . . and especially your legs . . . starting with your thighs . . . your knees . . . your calves . . . and your ankles . . . relax your feet . . . and even your toes just relax completely . . . as you begin to drift into a deep, relaxed state . . . just letting yourself go . . . just feeling good . . .

I would like you to use your imagination right now. Imagine yourself sitting comfortably in front of a large movie screen and imagine that you are seeing a motion picture of yourself. See it as vividly and in as much detail as possible. See yourself in this motion picture reacting successfully, in the ideal situation, having already attained your goal. As you are visualizing yourself as this successful person . . . see yourself as the main actor or lead person on your screen . . . How do you feel now that you have become the person that you would like to be? . . . (pause) . . . Feel the emotions . . . What are you feeling? . . . Maybe confidence . . . pride . . . fulfillment . . . satisfaction . . . relief . . . happiness . . . (pause) . . . What emotions are you feeling exactly? . . . Let those emotions fill you up . . . (pause) . . . Let them grow within you . . . (pause) . . . What are you hearing associated with your new goal? What are others maybe saying about you? How do they feel about your accomplishments? . . . (pause) . . . I'd also like you to visualize and feel what you think is different . . . What is different now that you have attained your goal? How has your life changed? . . . (pause) . . . Are you enjoying any more freedoms associated with this attainment?

What else is there that you can notice that is associated with this now orderly achievement? . . . See yourself for just a few more moments having achieved your new habit . . . (pause) . . .

You are in control of your life now . . . You have attained a new positive habit . . . With the power of your subconscious mind, it is very easy to do . . . You have allowed the past disorder to fade away like an unwanted memory . . . and now you move forward . . . The disorder of the past has been replaced with order. So once again feel that wonderful sense of satisfaction and achievement. It is coming from your strong subconscious mind. You have created your goal and through these daily exercises you are maintaining it, creating a permanent habit of change.

At the count of five you will come back to the here and now, feeling wonderful . . .

One . . . Beginning to come all the way back

Two . . . Coming back feeling better and better

Three . . . Feeling totally relaxed and comfortable

Four . . . Eyes starting to open now . . . and

Five . . . Eyes wide open, feeling wonderful in every way.

Chapter 6
How Thoughts Become Reality

Thoughts are the seeds of everything. They are a form of energy. Every moment of every day your thoughts are attracting similar energy to what you are sending out, whether you realize it or not. If you are thinking positive thoughts, you will attract more positive to you; if you are thinking negative thoughts, you will attract more negative to you. In this chapter you'll learn how this plays into hypnotism and how to get yourself on the road to a new and better you.

Imagination Versus Reality

Imagination is the ability to form mental images from your focused thoughts. There is a very strong correlation between imagination and reality. Thoughts *can* become things. W. Clement Stone stated it clearly when he said, "Whatever the mind of man can conceive and believe, it can achieve." What you say is not nearly as important as what you think and allow your mind to dwell on.

 **Question?**

What is the difference between visualization and imagination?
Visualization is when you are seeing something that you can relate to. It is something that may have already happened to you or that you understand from experience. Imagination is seeing something that has never happened to you and requires creativity.

The basis of hypnosis is imagination. In order for you to create health, wealth, or happiness in your mind, you must first imagine it. If you cannot imagine it in your mind, how can you create it in reality? If you can imagine it, you then have a blueprint to begin working with. Imagination gives you the picture or instructions of how you would like things to be.

Imagination in Health

Where are you placing your thoughts, focus, and attention? Are you placing them on health or sickness? Keep in mind that the subconscious mind does not understand negativity; therefore, if you are focusing on not being sick, your attention is being placed on "being sick." Instead, you must focus on being healthy. It is important to always focus on the positive aspects—what you want—rather than the negative aspects—what you don't want. You must be able to imagine yourself being healthy in order to be healthy. It is called the buying-in principle. If you cannot imagine it, then it is not believable to your subconscious mind.

If you want to be healthier, then imagine yourself as being a healthy person. Always imagine yourself as the end result of what you want to be. See yourself stronger and with more vigor. See yourself doing the things that you would be doing if you had the health that you desired. Focus on only the positive aspects. It is also important to correct your speech and say only positive things about your health. If someone asks you how you are, tell them you feel wonderful or better than ever.

Imagination in Wealth

Many people have a strong desire to be wealthy, and while they are hoping and desiring for this wealth, their minds are focused on their bills and where the money will come from to pay them. Even though there is a desire for wealth, their thoughts, focus, and attention are on their struggle; therefore, that is what they will attract.

In order to be wealthy your thoughts must be on wealth. You must be able to imagine yourself as a wealthy person and in a situation other than the one you are presently in. As the saying goes, "Seeing is believing." See the end result of your desires in your mind's eye.

Self-image is a big part of being successful. How do you feel about or identify yourself? Do you see yourself as worthy of success, or do you identify more as someone who can just never get ahead in life? In order to be successful you must see yourself as already being successful.

Why Self-Talk Alone Does Not Work

Positive self-talk has become more popular than ever before. You may even have attended a positive self-talk seminar, have audio or video courses at home, or have self-talk books on your shelves. Merely reading or reciting the positive self-talk is not effective. To achieve positive results, more is required.

Focus Imagination

Have you ever heard the saying, "Don't do what I say, do what I mean"? This is very similar to how positive self-talk affects the subconscious mind. Words alone have little effect on the subconscious until they are combined with pictures, imagination, or emotion. In other words, you can read or self-talk for a long period of time, but until there is focused attention placed on what you are saying or meaning attached to it, it will be of little effect. It's as if words alone are a separate language until the focus of imagination has been placed on them.

Have you ever listened to a lengthy lecture delivered in a monotone voice on a topic that you find of little interest? The words of the lecture simply fill the air, and you don't absorb the meaning unless the speaker begins to insert images, emotion, or excitement. Words alone are similar to having a textbook sitting on the table open to a page with no one reading it. Until there is focused attention of some sort, it is merely unused information.

Mindless Repetition

Another misconception of positive self-talk is that if it is repeated over and over it will become part of you. This is similar to the old-school stereotype of the teacher having her student write a sentence on a blackboard 200 times as a way of making him remember a lesson. Repetition without focus is a waste of time. Many times students trying to memorize answers for a test will read the answer over and over only to find that when the test began they could not remember the answer. If they had taken the time to create a picture with that same answer, chances are they would have remembered it. If they had also placed emotion within that picture and attached it to the answer, it would have come back to them even stronger.

Discover the Hidden Worlds Within

Everything in the world around you has a correlative in the world of thought. Everything from your desk, computer, this book, the chair you are sitting on, and even the cup you may be drinking from initially began as a thought.

Thoughts Become Things

The clothes you are wearing began as thought. Somewhere, someone had the thought of creating some new clothing. This thought was then acted upon with imagination. From that picture in the creator's mind came a design or the clothing itself. From that point someone else had the knowledge of how to mass-produce that clothing and through his imagination and the tools available to him proceeded to do so. Once the clothing was mass-produced, someone else had an initial thought of how to market the clothing, and through her thought process and imagination she was able to market the clothing to the location where you most likely purchased it. However, before you purchased it, you had a thought of wanting to purchase some clothing and had an idea of what you wanted. With this image in your mind, you went shopping and the clothing you purchased was the result.

Objects Are Copies of Thoughts

Everything you can imagine is a representation of an initial thought. It is sort of like a copy of the original, which was initially the thought. It is interesting to realize that it is not an exact copy. Think of the Taj Mahal. This is a spectacular palace that was built in Agra, India, and is world-renowned for its beauty. Shah Jahan dreamed it up as a memorial to his favorite wife, and it probably looked quite different in his mind than it does now. In his mind it was such a spectacular building that it may have had colors that were unimaginable. It may have had hundreds of spires, walkways, and levels, but then the imagined thoughts had to be placed on paper in a blueprint, which began to limit the imagination. Then with the tools available at that time, the present building known as the Taj Mahal was created. Even though it is magnificent, imagine how much more it must've been in the creator's mind.

 Question?

How can I change my thought process if I find it becoming negative?
You can utilize what is known as *thought stopping.* When you feel that a negative or unproductive line of thinking is happening, simply shout the word "stop" and you will create a break in that process. You must take that opportunity to immediately begin a new line of thinking.

Understanding Brain Wave States

Through the use of electroencephalographs, more commonly known as EEGs, electrical brain wave activity can be traced and monitored. The slower the brain wave state, the more open to suggestion or hypnosis you are. There are four major brain wave states: beta, alpha, theta, and delta.

Brain wave states are measured in hertz (Hz), which reflects the cycles per second of the electrical impulses that the brain produces. Your brain produces brain waves every moment of every day; however, at different times these waves will have different frequencies.

The Beta State

In your normal, everyday, busy activities you are in what is known as the beta state. This is your busy, working, thinking, decision-making state. As you are reading this book you are most likely in the beta state.

The Alpha State

As soon as you relax and close your eyes you are in what is known as the alpha state, which is a state of light relaxation. The alpha state is also the beginning of the hypnotic state. Alpha is a very simple state to attain and is a level of stress-free activity. This light state of hypnosis is adequate for most purposes, such as smoking cessation, weight loss, study habits, test taking, and the majority of the topics included in this book that do not require regression or pain management.

You may have noted that at the beginning of the self-hypnosis sessions presented in this book you are instructed to close your eyes and then take three deep breaths. The reason for this is to bring you to the alpha state quickly so suggestions can be given. The process of simply closing your eyes automatically blocks out approximately 80 percent of beta activity, and taking three deep breaths helps you reach the alpha state quite easily and quickly.

Fact

Alpha is also known as the earth or the animal state. This explains why when you are comfortably relaxed at home your pets tend to gravitate toward you more than at times when you are very busy in the beta state. Animals do not understand beta and are many times even annoyed by it.

The Theta State

The next level, the theta state, is the daydreaming state. This is also the brain wave level where suppressed memories are hidden. It is the level where your mind expands and is able to remember things more easily than other times. When you find yourself just falling off to sleep at night, you are in the theta state.

The Delta State

The delta state is a very deep state of relaxation where your brain wave activity has become extremely slow. It is also a place of accelerated healing and recuperation. While in the delta brain wave state, some people can undergo major surgery without the use of outside anesthesia.

You will still be able to hear suggestions and are able to react or resist if required while in the delta state. In most cases you will not be able to remember the suggestions given when you exit hypnosis. This is in no way a danger since if you did not like the suggestion being given, you would be able to simply open your eyes and state so.

The delta state is where the subconscious mind is able to expand beyond its physical parameters. It is a place of profound intuition and psychic ability. This is where most of the metaphysical aspects of hypnosis are conducted, such as remote viewing, astral projection, or out-of-body experiences. It is also known as the universal consciousness.

How to Make Changes Permanent

In order to create permanent change you must begin with changing your self-image. If your thoughts and memories of the past created the self-image that you presently have, then in order to change your self-image you must create new memories that will elevate your self-image. The way to create new memories is through the use of your imagination, because, as previously mentioned, the subconscious mind does not understand the difference between an imagined and a real memory.

Changing Your Mind

Maxwell Maltz, MD, author of *Psycho Cybernetics* and a plastic surgeon with New York hospitals, wrote of his extensive studies on the concept of self-image. Through his research, Maltz found that by giving subjects repeated positive input through guided imagery, hypnosis, or visualization, the subconscious minds of the subjects will create "engrams" (memory traces), which will produce new neuropathways. He found that the brain does not accept new data for a change unless it is repeatedly given each day for a minimum of twenty-one days (without missing a day). Only then can it become a habit.

It is important to reiterate that the same positive suggestions must be given each and every day for the entire twenty-one days. Due to the nature of the conscious mind, which rebels against change, if the repetition process is not continued, within approximately three to seven days you will return to your original behavior. This is why most hypnotic or positive-change programs usually include some sort of follow-up system.

Challenge Yourself

In order to make a change you must challenge yourself. The best gauges of realizing whether you are on track or not are your feelings. If you feel comfortable about the change that you are making, then you are probably not extending yourself enough. Change is not comfortable; in fact, it is inconvenient. It is important when creating a challenge for yourself that you think big. Creating a challenge that is bigger than your comfort zone can be a little scary, but it can also be exciting. If this is the case in your challenge, then go for it. You now have a worthy challenge. Making a big challenge is simply a way of getting you out of your comfort zone and striving for more than you think you can do. If you want to be someplace different tomorrow, you must do something different today.

Twenty-One Days for Change

Through the use of your imagination you can now use self-hypnosis to create positive change in your life. This same program can be used to change virtually any disorder that you desire. Although you may find that the desired change occurs after just one session, keep in mind that in order to maintain that change as a permanent habit you must continue for the entire twenty-one days.

How to Use the Twenty-One-Day Program

The twenty-one-day for change program can be used with any of the self-help topics in this book. Here is how the program works. First you must decide on the topic that you would like to hypnotize yourself for. Then insert your script in your desired template depending on whether you prefer an analytical or nonanalytical session. Utilizing whichever form of self-hypnosis you choose, listen to that session for the first day. Once the specific suggestions are put into your subconscious mind, they will remain there permanently and your desired positive change has been made as long as you were not rebelling against the suggestions.

In order for this change to remain permanent, listen to the follow-up session found in Chapter 5 in the section titled Follow Up for Success. Listen to this exact same session each and every day starting with day two and for the remaining nineteen days.

Alert!

During the follow-up session, each day you will be asked to use your imagination and imagine yourself as having already attained your goal. Once you have created the image, it is important to keep the exact same image for each of the twenty-one days without changing it.

Use It for Other Topics

Once you have completed the twenty-one days and you have attained your goal, you can then move on to the next topic you would like to be hypnotized for and use the follow-up session with that topic. The twenty-one-day program can be used for any area of self-improvement. Once you have used it for all of your issues, have your spouse try it for her issues.

Fact

The interesting thing with this program is that it does not require deep hypnosis or even going into hypnosis at all for it to be successful. All that it requires is that you use your imagination to see yourself as successful in whatever topic you choose. The active ingredient is your imagination.

The reason that this works so well is that you know more about how you would like to see yourself in the completed goal better than anyone else. Using this program, you may find that several issues will be improved at the same time rather than just the one you were focusing on. Be careful, however, not to use it for more than one main topic at a time so as not to overwhelm your subconscious mind.

Chapter 7
Common Misconceptions Clarified

When you think of hypnosis, your mind may conjure up this mysterious, often evil, dominating character with dark sinister eyes that has an unbelievable magical power. Thoughts of being taken advantage of, overpowered, or tricked in some way race through your mind. These are a few of the many misconceptions about hypnosis. This chapter explodes some of those myths and presents the positive side of hypnosis.

Myth 1: Only Weak-Minded People Can Be Hypnotized

Anyone with reasonable intelligence can be hypnotized. Since the basis of hypnosis is being open to suggestion, if you are able to read and understand simple instructions, you are able to be hypnotized. Hypnosis is similar to a set of instructions to build something. If the instructions are followed, it works. If they are not, then the desired effect will not take place.

 Alert!

Younger children may not be hypnotizable due to their inability to sit still and focus. If, however, they are old enough to understand the language spoken, they can still be hypnotized in a process called *sleep hypnosis*, where they are gently taken out of sleep to the point where they are not totally alert and then given suggestions.

You can be hypnotized if you have a strong or a weak mind. You can be hypnotized if you have your eyes opened or closed. You can even be hypnotized if you cannot hear.

Although anyone can be hypnotized, anyone can also resist hypnosis. The only requirement is the desire to be hypnotized (or not), plus an understanding of what you need to do in order to achieve the hypnotic state. The level of hypnosis, however, varies according to a person's willingness to let go.

Myth 2: Hypnosis Is Sleep

Although the word *hypnosis* was derived from the Greek god of sleep, Hypnos, hypnosis is nothing like sleep. In hypnosis your mind is focused and in most cases alert. You are very aware of what is going on around you. You are actually in a state of what is called *hypersensitivity*. All of your senses and emotions are enhanced. It is closer to a state of daydreaming or relaxation. You are focused on the words of the hypnotherapist, and outside sounds seem to fade away.

 *Question?*

If my subconscious mind is always working, why can't I sleep during a session?
During a hypnosis session, while you are awake your mind is focused on the instructions being given as well as on the concern that you have. When you are sleeping your subconscious mind is unfocused and more passive.

During a session, most subjects will find the deep relaxation so enjoyable that they will not allow themselves to fall asleep as they do not want to miss it. In the rare case that you do fall asleep, the hypnotist can easily wake you in a gentle manner so as to finish the session rather than let you sleep, or in a self-hypnosis session you'll simply wake up after a brief nap.

Myth 3: Hypnosis Is a Truth Serum

Due to the way hypnosis is portrayed in society today, people are afraid that they will tell a hypnotist all of their deep, dark secrets. They are worried that they may divulge their checking account numbers or tell where they have money buried in their backyard while in a deep trance.

Hypnosis is not a truth serum; in fact, it is more the opposite. You are a better liar in hypnosis. The reason for that is while you are relaxed you are able to retrieve information from your subconscious mind more readily and therefore have more knowledge at your fingertips than you would normally. Also, since you are more relaxed you would appear to be truthful while telling a lie.

Confabulation

Confabulation is a phenomenon where a subject under hypnosis makes something up, either knowingly or unknowingly, in response to a question. An example of this is a subject who is extremely relaxed and asked to remember information from a hit-and-run accident. While the subject is attempting to recreate his steps and what he saw, the hypnotherapist begins to ask him questions that he cannot presently answer. Due to the extreme relaxation and enjoyable feeling of hypnosis, a subject may become frustrated due to the barrage of questions and may give answers that are not true just to appease the hypnotherapist.

Confabulation can be done unknowingly. Keep in mind that everything you have ever experienced in your life is stored in perfect clarity in your subconscious mind. Even though you may think that many incidents from your childhood have been forgotten, they are still there in your subconscious. So if you are under hypnosis and are asked a question, there is always the chance that you may come up with some elaborate story with very specific details that you believe actually did happen but may have simply been something that happened in your childhood or even something that you watched on television from your childhood.

Fact

> Due to the possibility of confabulation, testimony attained or given while under the influence of hypnosis is not admissible in a court of law in most states. Although the information gathered may not be admissible in court, in many instances it has been used to help law enforcement officials solve crimes.

Myth 4: You Won't Hear Everything Being Said

You will hear everything that is being said in a hypnosis session while it is being said. Your hearing, as well as all of your senses, is enhanced tremendously due to the extreme relaxation and lack of distraction. Many times in hypnosis you may even hear conversations that are occurring outside the room you are being hypnotized in.

Even though you are hearing everything that is being said, as it is being said, you may not remember what was said at the end of the session. Depending on how deeply relaxed you are, at certain levels of hypnosis your memory can be affected to the point that when you emerge from hypnosis you will not remember anything or very little that occurred during the session. This is known as the amnesia level. It is the same depth of hypnosis that someone is brought to for the purpose of anesthesia. Keep in mind that even though you may not remember what happened during the session, you are still in control and have a choice while the suggestions are been given.

 Essential

It is interesting to note that while in a room filled with people speaking, the conscious mind can only effectively concentrate on or understand one conversation at a time. In hypnosis, however, the conscious mind is able to understand and distinguish multiple conversations simultaneously. This, in fact, is the premise that many subliminal hypnotic programs are based on.

Myth 5: You'll Be Forced to Do Things Against Your Will

You will not do anything that is against your nature or personal standards. You cannot be made to violate your own values or accepted patterns of behavior. You would either reject the suggestion or come out of hypnosis. You hear everything that is said. You are in complete control at all times.

Television programs often portray people under hypnosis becoming assassins or doing evil things. First of all, keep in mind that it is television, which is supposed to be entertaining. As the previous paragraph stated, you would not do anything against your nature or personal standards. So if you are inherently a very good person, you could not be turned into an assassin or an evil person in hypnosis unless you wanted to be. However, if you are already a very negative person who is not beyond doing these types of things, then it is possible. Hypnosis will not make you do anything you do not want to; however, if you *do* want to do something, even if it is negative or harmful, hynosis will help you to be even better at what you wish to do.

Myth 6: You'll Get Stuck in Hypnosis

The hypnotic state can be terminated at any time you chose. No matter how deep in hypnosis you are, if you had an urge to go to the bathroom, you can open your eyes and excuse yourself so you could go. You are always under your own control.

It's your choice to enter the hypnotic state, and you can always choose to leave it. If you were left in a deep hypnotic state by your hypnotherapist who decided to leave the room to go to lunch during the middle of your session, you would either return to full consciousness on your own or enter a natural sleep and awaken after a short pleasant nap.

There is no trance and you are not under anyone's power. That is merely Hollywood. There has never been a terminal case of hypnosis in the emergency room. Zombies are not under any type of hypnotic trance; they are fictitious characters.

 Fact

The deepest state of hypnosis, which remains a mystery to most, is known as the hypno-coma state. This is a state of hypnosis that is so wonderful that even the sound of the hypnotherapist's voice is an annoyance and is often ignored by the client. It is also a state where the body seems to heal at an excessively higher speed.

On occasion there have been hypnotherapists, especially new ones to the field, who have reported that their clients had become stuck in hypnosis and they were not able to get them out of that state for several minutes and sometimes even longer. The reason for this condition is not that a subject was stuck, rather the subject was excessively relaxed and chose to remain there out of enjoyment. She chose to keep her eyes closed, but if the hypnotherapist told the client that he would leave her there for another hour and that he charges $200 per hour, the client would immediately open her eyes. Money, at times, can be a great motivator.

Myth 7: There Are Too Many Dangers and Side Effects

There are no known negative side effects in conjunction with going into hypnosis. Hypnosis is no more dangerous than relaxing in your favorite recliner. The only side effect to hypnosis is relaxation. It does not cause stroke, seizures, sickness, or stress. However, if you are prone to seizures (or any other malady), it can occur even in hypnosis just as it may during sleep.

Suggestibility is not dangerous as you are always in control. It is similar to being a carpenter and having a toolbox stocked with whatever you need to build a house. The tools in your box are not dangerous by themselves, but they can be used by some unscrupulous person for dangerous purposes. Hypnosis, in a similar vein, could be abused by someone who had an evil ulterior motive. If someone were a good enough conman in real life, he may also be able to fool or mislead you into doing something bad in hypnosis. Anyone, of course, can be tricked, but you have the comfort of knowing that in hypnosis your faculties are heightened and you would most likely have better judgment and restraint.

Myth 8: Hypnosis Is a Magical Spell

This misconception is probably the most damaging to those who desire to benefit from hypnosis. Hypnosis is not a magic spell. It is simply a helpmate. There is nothing taking control over your body, making you change against your will.

The mystery of hypnosis is that it is a helpful tool in attaining goals but cannot be seen or touched. Some in the medical community refer to it as clinical even though it is totally of the mind and powered by thought and imagination. Something difficult to understand or rationalize within the conscious mind often gets labeled as magic or even a miracle. It's interesting to note that many miracles of the past can be explained with science or are commonplace occurrences today. Many of the advanced medical techniques used in hospitals today may have also been considered magic years ago.

Rather than being a magic spell, hypnosis simply assists you in your progress. Being a helpmate requires participation on your part. It requires desire and commitment. Once you are committed to change and are ready to take the next step, it is there to help you through the use of your strong subconscious mind. It is your own subconscious mind that is doing the work, not some mysterious outside magical influence.

Chapter 8
Roadblocks to Permanent Change

In addition to the conscious mind being a creature of habit and wishing things to remain the status quo, there are many other roadblocks or hindrances to success that you should be aware of. These hindrances include stress, fear, past memories, victimization, and negative self-image. This chapter will help you to identify, understand, and restore your growth process.

The Many Faces of Stress

Stress is a common factor behind disorders such as heart attack, stroke, depression, and even skin irritation. Here are some of the most common triggers of stress and what can be done to alleviate them.

Stress does not exist in the alpha brain wave state; it is a beta brain wave activity. By simply closing your eyes you are blocking out approximately 80 percent of beta activity. This will greatly reduce your stress on the spot. Adding three deep breaths in addition to closing your eyes will reduce your stress even more.

Overexaggerating

When encountering a stressful situation, many people think of the worst-case scenario, which then causes them more stress. This leads to a domino effect, causing the stress to spiral even deeper. For example, say your employer asks you to come to his office at two o'clock concerning a project you have been working on. You begin to worry and think about the worst possibilities of what he might have to say. Things begin to race through your mind, such as "What if he doesn't like my work?" "Will I get fired?" "If I get fired, will I have enough money to pay my bills?" "What in the world will I do?"

When you find yourself in this situation, identify your problem and actually think it through. If the boss, for example, was unsatisfied with your work, perhaps all he would do is have you redo it. On the other hand, maybe he just wants to give you praise. By working it through you may find that the outcomes were less severe than what you initially imagined, causing less stress.

Improper Diet

Many foods can have a negative impact on your emotional and physical health by causing large sweeping mood swings. Alcohol, sugar, and caffeine are particularly known to increase stress.

In addition to the foods you eat, notice your eating environment. Are you eating on the run, in your car while driving, while watching television, or on the computer? Taking the time to relax while eating and focusing on your meal will help eliminate stress.

 Alert!

Before making any major changes in your diet or deciding to take vitamins or supplements, check with a qualified medical professional or nutritionist for advice and guidance. A lack of certain vitamins in your diet can cause anger and stress. Getting and following proper nutritional advice from a qualified professional can help you lower stress and anger levels.

Chronic Pain

Chronic pain causes stress because you are not able to accomplish ordinary tasks that you were previously able to do. This can cause feelings of inadequacy or of being left out, which in turn can cause feelings of stress and even depression.

Excessive Demands or Deadlines

Excessive demands or deadlines are a common source of stress. Many people create deadlines and procrastinate habitually, which can create stress. Things can begin to pile up, and suddenly something very small can cause a person to become overwhelmed. Deep breathing is an excellent stress reliever in this situation, as is dedicating a few moments to relaxing self-hypnosis.

Eliminating Fear and Guilt

Fear of the unknown, such as the results of what may happen from being late for work, taking a test, or giving a business presentation, can create stress. Receiving a bill that may be larger than you can presently handle can also cause undue stress. Fear, in many cases, takes on a life of its own.

The Boogieman or Shadows of Fear

Sometimes fear disguises itself as the boogieman hiding in the closet or scary shadows against the wall. The fear that you have is an illusion and in many cases is something that will never even take place. It is a scenario that has played in your mind of what could happen, not what is happening. It is a projection.

Focusing on the present is a great solution in these cases. Instead of fearing what could happen, such as if you do not have the money to pay for that upcoming bill, focus on what is happening right now. Right now you are safe, comfortable, have food to eat, and a place to stay. Life is okay at this moment, and much can happen before the specific time of reckoning to change it. An unexpected check can come in, or you can receive a bonus at work, make a sale of a product, or even make payment arrangements with the bill collector.

 Essential

One way to eliminate stress is to describe out loud in as much detail as possible a picture that you are looking at. Do it as if you were describing it to someone over the phone who was trying to recreate it perfectly. This exercise requires you to concentrate on the present task at hand and will eliminate your stress.

To eliminate the shadow that is haunting you, think of your fear as an illusion, which you can dismiss by thinking of the present. It's as easy as turning on the light switch to eliminate a shadow.

The Infection of Guilt

Guilt is an issue from the past that can hinder your progress in moving ahead. Guilt acts more as an infection in life rather than an emotion. Having guilt hinders the feeling of emotions such as love, happiness, or excitement. Many times it leaves you feeling empty.

Guilt arises due to the result of making a decision. One of the ways to alleviate guilt is to think back to the decision you made that created the guilt. Once you have determined the cause, simply decide to undecide. Rethink the decision you made and examine the reasons why you came to that specific conclusion and then correct them.

Leaving the Past Behind

Many people cling to their experiences and limitations of the past as a way of having an excuse not to move forward. This is only excess baggage that slows you down.

Approximately 90 percent of all decisions are decided as a result of your past and only 10 percent are a result of the actual situation. Challenge someone to walk across a wood beam that is elevated approximately five feet in the air. If the person being challenged had never fallen before, she would most likely take the challenge and happily walk across. If someone else taking the challenge had fallen and gotten hurt due to a similar incident, he would most likely decline the challenge.

It seems like the past is always lingering somewhere in your mind to effect your present and future. When given a challenge, you may have heard people respond with statements such as, "I'm not very coordinated, I probably won't be able to do that." "I've never been able to do anything like that before." "That kind of thing has never worked for me." Each one of these statements is an excuse from the past to not have to attempt something in the present. They are self-imposed limitations that can be crippling.

 Essential

> In order to understand the nature of fear, look at fear as an acronym: False Evidence Appearing Real. Fear is something that exists in your mind that has not happened, or it is something from the past that has created a life or reality of its own.

Being aware of this hindrance is the first step toward progress. Through awareness you can attempt to leave the past behind you so that you can approach each challenge in life as a unique, new challenge. You can now make decisions with the information at hand rather than relying on limitations of your past. Whenever you find yourself using a past experience as a reason not to confront a new challenge, realize that it is an excuse.

Playing the Victim Game

If you are not taking 100 percent responsibility for your life, you are playing the victim game. There are three major activities that the victim indulges in: blame, justification, and complaining. Playing the victim game is an excuse to not have to achieve. It takes away the responsibility of the individual and also the stress of failure.

Blame

People who play the victim game are notorious for placing the blame on others for their problems or failures. They find someone else to point the finger at rather than accepting responsibility. They will say that the reason they are the way they are is the fault of their spouse, family, parents, religion, society, employer, or even the government. They are either a victim or the target of a victimizer.

Justify

People who justify tend to say things like "Being healthy isn't important to me." If health were not important to them, then they would not be seeking it. They might not want to be inconvenienced by having to exercise, eat healthy, or do what it takes, and it is easier to justify their actions by denying their desire for it.

Fact

By eliminating excuses from your vocabulary and taking responsibility for your actions, you will find that you can retake control of your life. A new terminology you can use is to "be straight" in your dealings and speech. If you say and do what you really mean, then there is no reason for excuses.

Another justification is, "I don't really need money anyway." This is a classic for those who cannot get a job or do not want to work for whatever reason. It is a justification of what they cannot acquire. Remember the basic rule when utilizing thought and your imagination: whatever you place your thoughts, focus, and attention on you attract to you. If you focus on not needing money, then that is exactly what you will get, no money.

Complain

People who chronically complain tend to think they have rough lives. They have a "woe is me" attitude. They are attracting more of what they are complaining about to themselves. The negative, complaining type of energy is very contagious, and those who indulge in this activity often seek out the companionship of others who also complain. In fact, complainers seem to enjoy listening to each other and will anxiously wait for their turn to complain about what is negative in their lives.

Victims enjoy getting attention as they confuse getting attention with love. Many times they misinterpret love as what others can do for them or give to them. They feel that the way to be deserving or worthy of love is through "buying" it.

Identifying and Replacing Habits

Every habit that you have began at one time as a choice you made. Once you have identified the habit that you would like to change, then the next step is to replace that habit. It is important to realize that a habit cannot be eliminated; it must be replaced with another habit that is hopefully a positive one.

Choices

Self-sabotage is a habit as well as a choice. Success is a habit as well as a choice. Insecurity is a habit as well as a choice. Confidence is a habit as well as a choice. Every habit began as a choice and through repetition became a habit. We all have habits, some of them positive and others not.

 Fact

> Even when you play the victim game by blaming, justifying, or complaining, that behavior began with a choice and through repetition became a habit. You can also make a new choice of being responsible for yourself and through repetition can rid yourself of being the victim.

Habits are initially created through your thoughts and are reinforced through repetition combined with past experiences. Everything you have experienced in your past has made you the person that you are today. Your past experiences have given you your present self-image.

Anything can become a habit through repetition. Some of the habits that you have created through repetition might be riding a bicycle, driving a car, saying "bless you" when someone sneezes, typing, and maybe even taking off your hat when you enter a house. Through continued repetition, just about anything, whether it is positive or negative, could become a habit.

Where Is Your Focus?

Two people who had the same opportunities can have entirely different habits due to the choices they made. They could be the exact same age, enjoy the same hobbies, attend the same schools and get the same degrees, live in the same city, and even work at the same job. Even with all these similarities, one can create a habit of being angry and living a meager life while the other can create a habit of being rich and happy. Yes, being rich is a habit that begins as a choice.

 Essential

> Rather than looking at situations in your life as problems, look at them as opportunities. Think about how you can approach this new opportunity to learn something, grow from it, or maybe even help someone. Break it down to see what positive can come from it and accomplish it the best you can.

What can make these two people so different, even after having lived virtually an identical life? One of the most evident differences would be in playing the victim game. One obviously decided to be the victim, allowing life's situations to control his life, while the other decided to take 100 percent responsibility and take control of his life. There is no such thing as a truly successful victim.

Desire

In order to replace a habit, once it has been acknowledged, you must have a desire to change. Although self-hypnosis will be the strongest help you may have ever had in your personal progress, it will not be successful by itself. Self-hypnosis is not a magic spell; it requires a strong desire or commitment on your end as well.

 **Question?**

How can I buy into something when my goal is so far away or huge?
If a goal is too big to seem attainable right now, all you need to do is break it down into smaller goals. Once you attain the lower increment, simply proceed to the next portion until you have finally accomplished your goal in its entirety.

Here is where the buying-in principle comes into play. In order to change in any area of your life, you must be able to believe that the change is possible. You must be able to imagine it. In other words, if you wanted to run a marathon but have difficulty running from your front door to the mailbox, then you have not satisfied the buying-in principle. If you cannot imagine yourself doing something, there will be no change.

How Do You See Yourself?

When you describe yourself to someone else, do you think of yourself as a successful, healthy, and positive person, or do you identify yourself more as a negative, self-sabotaging, unsuccessful person? However you answer this question, that is your self-image.

Self-Image

You can never exceed your self-image for very long. You may try to behave as someone that you are not; however, before long you will ultimately snap back to who you perceive yourself to be. It's as if your life were tethered to a bungee cord. No matter how many times you stretch it, the bungee will ultimately pull you back to where you began unless you change your self-image.

 Essential

Many people have a distorted image of how they see themselves, similar to looking into a warped carnival mirror. Others may not see you as you see yourself. All of your abilities, actions, feelings, and behaviors will always be consistent with your self-image. You will always act like the kind of person that you perceive yourself to be.

This explains the yo-yo syndrome. You can see this most often with people trying to quit smoking, lose weight, or even get off of drugs. If you are trying to quit smoking but still perceive yourself as a smoker who has quit for several months, you will spring back to being a smoker sometime down the road. The reason for this is that you must change your self-image in order to create a new habit so you can identify yourself as a nonsmoker.

Overnight Sensations

Overnight sensations are common in the entertainment industry. There have been many newly discovered movie stars who have become millionaires virtually overnight. Looking at these stars from an outside vantage point, it would seem that they are living a dream life and have everything a person would want. However, in many cases, within a short period of time many of these stars squander their money away. Or you will read in the newspapers of stars resorting to drugs, crime, destructive behavior, and even suicide. The reason is that even though they were given millions of dollars, their self-image may have been that of a self-sabotaging or undeserving person.

Ⓔ *Alert!*

It takes preparation to be successful. Are you prepared to receive whatever it is you want should you actually receive it? Being prepared to receive your goals of riches or happiness is the first and vital step in success. Take the time to determine your possible roadblocks and remove them.

On the other hand, you may have heard of people who, due to their positive, winning self-image, have propelled themselves from rags to riches in no time. It seems that no matter how many times adversity gets thrown at them they always seem to land on their feet and continue to be successful.

Chapter 9
The Big Six Broken Down

This chapter focuses on six of the most common self-hypnosis topics and will help you understand them more clearly. Although self-hypnosis is highly successful in other areas (see Chapters 10–13), the following six areas have seen a lot of success and gained in popularity.

Smoking Cessation

The majority of smokers who try to stop have been smoking on average between five and thirty-five years. Anything that is done for this length of time is a deeply engrained habit. The following section will give you the assistance that you need to break that habit and replace it with a new one of health if you truly have a desire to quit.

Helpful Tips

Before beginning your smoking cessation program, there are a few preparations that you should do. First, dispose of any smoking paraphernalia such as cigarettes, ashtrays, lighters, matches. Even though you may have other uses for lighters and matches, such as lighting candles or your gas stove, it is important that you get new ones and destroy the ones that you used for smoking. The reason for this is that each time you use the same lighter that you used for smoking you are sending yourself subconscious triggers, reminding you that this is the same lighter you use for smoking and possibly causing more cravings.

 Fact

Drinking water whenever you have a craving will also help you to flush out your system quicker as well as help you to not gain weight. The reason most people gain weight when they quit smoking is that they replace their smoking habit with a habit of eating rather than drinking water.

Next, replace any ashtray throughout the house with a bottle or a glass of water for the next week. If at any time after you have quit smoking you walk by where you used to have an ashtray and begin to get a craving, simply take eight deep breaths and a sip of water for the craving to go away. The purpose of this is to create a new habit that will replace the old one. Taking eight deep breaths will deliver more oxygen within your system, which will help you relax. Relaxation is one of the top reasons why most people state that they smoke. By taking a sip of water, you are replacing the bad habit of smoking with a good habit of drinking water.

The most important thing that will help you remain a nonsmoker is to hypnotize yourself utilizing the follow-up session for an additional twenty days after listening to the following smoking cessation session. Keep in mind that just listening to a session once does not create a habit. A habit is developed through repetition.

Alert!

Clean out your ashtray in your vehicle if you used that for smoking. You should not just empty it; it should be cleaned out well so the car does not have the smell of cigarettes in it.

Smoking Cessation Script

You have decided to quit smoking . . . and the way that you are going to quit smoking, right now, is simply to relax . . . that's right, you're going to slow down, relax, and just let everything go . . . and take this time . . . that you've chosen for yourself . . . to feel totally at ease . . . you have no place else to be right now . . . and nothing else to do . . . so just let everything go . . . and take this time that you've chosen to be here . . . to be completely relaxed . . .

You have a strong desire to stop smoking . . . You have decided that today is the day . . . Today is the day to be a nonsmoker once and for all . . . To become a nonsmoker . . . in just a few moments . . . your goal will be reached . . . you will be a nonsmoker . . . you will have stopped smoking . . . once and for all . . . and you'll never smoke again . . . So as time passes by . . . think of yourself in the following way . . . You are a nonsmoker . . . You have stopped smoking . . . and you will never smoke again . . . and as a nonsmoker you have the ability to be around other people who smoke . . . You have the ability to enjoy life as a nonsmoker . . . everything you do . . . from this moment on . . . is better as a nonsmoker . . . it doesn't matter whether you're at home . . . at work . . . alone or with others . . . you are in control . . . Everything is so much more enjoyable as a nonsmoker.

Just allow a wonderful feeling of confidence to move through you right now . . . at this very moment . . . realizing that you are a nonsmoker . . . feel the confidence that you now have overcome that negative habit . . . you have reached your goal and become a nonsmoker . . . here and now.

It is important to realize that to accomplish anything worthwhile in your life . . . you must give it 100 percent effort . . . and to remain a nonsmoker is no different . . . By giving it 100 percent you have made a commitment to win . . . You have stopped smoking . . . you are a nonsmoker . . . and you will never smoke again . . . from this moment on . . . your desire . . . your commitment . . . is stronger than ever before.

You are beginning a new positive habit . . . one that will help you in every part of your life . . . you'll find that from this moment forward . . . that water will taste better to you than ever before . . . that crisp, refreshing water will quench your thirst like it never has . . . that life-giving water will help you in every step of the way to become healthier . . . you have overcome a negative habit and are replacing it with this new, positive habit of drinking water.

Now that you have stopped smoking, you'll find that you have more energy, energy that will be needed to be put to good use . . . You'll find yourself being able to move easier . . . feeling better about yourself . . .

You are a nonsmoker now! . . . You have stopped smoking . . . and you will never smoke again.

Weight Loss

Overeating is one of the most prevalent addictions in the United States today. With other addictions, such as smoking and drug use, it is possible after quitting to never go back to using those substances again. There is simply no possibility of that when it comes to eating. Eating is something that you must do on a regular basis to remain alive.

The Diet Label

Due to the rebellious nature of the conscious mind, it is very important to never label what you are doing a not think you can eliminate it completely for a week, challenge yourself to cut dramatically the amount of servings you consume. After the first week, challenge yourself with a different item for another week. Continue to do this for at least three weeks with other items on your list. Since this is only a one-week challenge, and you are able to have that item afterward, the rebellion will be very little and your weight loss will begin with a jumpstart.

Weight Loss Script

Starting right now . . . You no longer have the urge to overeat or to snack in between meals . . . Because healthy, well-balanced meals more than satisfy your appetite . . . and the taste and aroma of your food are better than ever before . . . Rich, heavy, sweet, fattening foods and drink just no longer appeal to you . . . Because healthy, life-giving foods taste wonderful and fill you up.

You noticeably eat your food slower . . . Chewing it thoroughly . . . You put down your fork in between bites and don't pick it up again until the bite in your mouth is gone . . .

You will be drinking water more than ever before . . . water will be there to help you lose weight and to remain healthy. That wonderful crisp, clear refreshing water will taste great to you . . . You'll find yourself craving water more and more each and every day . . .

You only eat healthy meals and do not become hungry in between meals . . . You do not want to stuff yourself because you'll feel so much healthier and vigorous without an uncomfortable, over-filled stomach . . . You will eat until you are satisfied, not until you are stuffed.

"diet." The very nature of the word *diet* in many cases causes the conscious mind to rebel. If you think of the conscious mind as a creature of habit that does not want to change at all, you can see the resistance that occurs when hearing the word *diet*. Dieting means that you must change your eating habits. It requires you to eat different than you have before in order to create a positive change

Challenge Yourself

Although the word *diet* creates panic due to its sense of permanency, you may use the word *challenge* with little resistance. Take a moment to establish what the main food culprits are that keep you from being at your goal weight. Choose at least the top three. Most lists include foods such as pastas, breads, chips, fried foods, and sweets.

 Essential

When reading the script onto your recording device, it can be advantageous to stress or accent some of the action words as a way to drive them home. You can do this by saying the specific words or word in a slightly louder or convicted tone similar to how some television evangelists do in their sermons to make a point.

Once you have determined your three biggest prits, take one item on your list, such as potato chips, challenge yourself not to eat any for one week. If you

You'll not lose weight so quickly that it will harm your health, but you will lose weight in a steady, constant manner . . . and you'll find that you have more energy . . . Energy that will be needed to be put to good use . . . Everything you do will become easier . . . and you will want to do more each and every day to increase your health.

Each meal that you eat, you'll leave a small portion of food on your plate that you will then throw away once you are finished . . . As you find yourself doing this, more and more you'll find that portion you left on your plate becomes larger . . . This will aid you in eating less . . . It will give you great confidence to know that you can walk away, leaving food on your plate . . . confidence that will continue to grow more and more as you proceed toward your goal.

You are in control of yourself and have taken the first step in controlling your eating habits.

Relieving Insomnia

In today's busy world, more and more people are suffering from insomnia than ever before. The proof of this is the many products sold in pharmacies for insomnia as well as the many commercials on television. Lack of sleep often increases stress, anxiety, and frustration that in turn can lead to many more serious illnesses.

Busy Minds

Many people find that they have to work many more hours than ever before to make a living and oftentimes do not take a break or have any downtime before sleeping. The problem with this is that while they are lying in bed attempting to sleep, their minds are still on the business of their workday, contemplating what they've done and planning what they are going to do the next day. Their minds are so busy that they are not able to let go and focus on relaxing.

Focusing to Let Go

Two things that are imperative in order to fall asleep are letting go and focusing. One of the best ways to let go is to create a schedule where you can have at least an hour or two to yourself so you unwind before going to bed. A good way to do this is to sit in a quiet room and listen to inspirational music. You could also make some time to read an enjoyable novel. Whatever you choose, make it something enjoyable and different from work.

 Fact

Counting sheep to fall asleep does not work because you are counting forward, which is never ending. If you want this to work, you must start with a fixed amount of sheep (such as 100) and then count backward slowly. Condition your mind that when it becomes too tiring or bothersome to count that you simply stop and allow yourself to sleep.

Focusing is a wonderful technique to guide you into sleep. When most people suffer from insomnia, their minds are thinking of many things all at once, making it very difficult to let go and sleep. By focusing on only one item, such as counting backward slowly from 100 down to one, their minds must focus on the task at hand in order to accomplish it, thereby pushing everything else out. Allow yourself to focus on this test until it becomes too tiring and you allow yourself to drift off to sleep.

You must continually tell yourself that you will sleep easily and comfortably this evening. Your subconscious mind responds to what you say consciously and believe. Therefore, if you go to bed this evening saying to yourself, "I won't be able to sleep again tonight," that is exactly what your subconscious mind will make happen. So be positive, open-minded, and believe that it is possible to sleep easily when you go to bed.

Insomnia Scripts—Focusing Technique

NOTE: The following insomnia script does not need to be inserted within the other portions of the session. It is self-contained and can be recorded just as it is.

Get comfortable in your bed in a position in which you are ready to go to sleep . . . close your eyes . . . take a deep breath, and exhale and relax . . . take a second deep breath . . . and as you exhale . . . let go of any tension . . . or stress that you may have . . . and now take a third deep breath . . . hold it for three seconds . . . and exhale and relax.

You have a desire to sleep through the night . . . to sleep easily . . . to get to sleep quickly . . . and to stay asleep until morning . . . and the way you are going to do this . . . starting right now . . . is to learn the proper way to focus your way to sleep.

The way that you are going to do this is by learning to focus your mind on one item . . . or one task . . . by using your imagination . . . I would like you to imagine right now that you are in your bed, and you are more comfortable than you have ever been before . . . It is as if you are lying on the most comfortable feather bed you can imagine . . . Imagine what it would feel like to be in this large, thick comfortable feather bed . . . Imagine that you are now looking up and you realize that there is no ceiling there . . . instead you are able to look outside into the evening sky . . . You notice that there is a full moon out and you are able to see very clearly . . . It is a comfortable evening . . . and the temperature is just right . . . Even though you are able to see outside into the sky you realize that it is very comfortable and very safe . . . As you're looking up into the sky you notice a cloud pushed by a gentle wind moving overhead . . . As you focus on the cloud you notice that it seems to form into the shape of the number ninety-nine . . . Notice it closely as you see the numbers form . . . You notice it for a few seconds and then the wind seems to blow the number ninety-nine away . . . and then you notice the clouds forming above your head into the number ninety-eight . . . Take some time to see the number ninety-eight form completely . . . Now you see the number ninety-eight blow away . . . and then another cloud forms overhead turning into the shape of the number ninety-seven . . . Once again the gentle wind blows it away . . . As I am speaking, you notice that this pattern continues as the clouds form into the number ninety-six . . . then blows away . . . going slowly, as you continually watch and focus on these clouds forming into the next number going downward in sequence . . . forming into a number ninety-five . . . then blowing away and continuing on and on . . . I would like you to continue watching the clouds from this point forward on your own . . . paying no further attention to me . . . or any outside sounds . . . Watch the next cloud form . . . See it clearly for a few seconds . . . and then fade away . . . paying no more attention to my voice . . . just watching the next cloud . . . and the next one . . . going down further and further . . . With every cloud you see approach . . . and every cloud that blows away . . . you will go deeper and deeper into relaxation . . . With every cloud that forms and every cloud that goes away you will become more sleepy . . . more drowsy . . . as you can, let go of everything that has happened during the day . . . and just focus on your clouds . . . until you get to the point . . . where focusing on the clouds . . . and counting them downward . . . becomes simply too tiring . . . too much of a hindrance . . . or too inconvenient . . . and when that happens . . . you may just stop counting . . . and allow yourself to drop off . . . into a deep . . . sound sleep . . . and you will find . . . that when you drop off into this deep . . . sound . . . sleep . . . that you will be able to sleep until morning . . . without any interruptions . . . without anything disturbing you . . . unless there is something that is in need of your immediate attention . . . and should that happen . . . you will take care of the situation . . . and when you go back to bed . . . you'll be able to fall deeply into sleep again . . . very quickly . . . All outside sounds . . . fade away completely . . . as you continue to count down . . . so much deeper . . . you'll find that you'll become sleepy . . . just by thinking of this exercise . . . you will be able to go to sleep on your own . . . very easily . . . because now you understand . . . the secrets . . . the procedures . . . of how to go to sleep . . . It is simply by focusing on one thing . . . and letting go of all the busy tasks . . . of the day . . . Whatever you haven't finished today . . . will still be there tomorrow . . . Keeping your mind on it . . . or thinking of it . . . is not helping you to get the job done . . . or helping you to sleep . . . You must let go of the business of the day . . . and focus on sleep . . . focus on these clouds . . . as you continue to count down . . . each

cloud . . . and eventually . . . it becomes tiresome . . . and you let go
. . . into sleep . . . you may be feeling . . . like you want to let go now .
. . or very . . . very soon . . . You may have let go already . . . and are
just listening . . . to the sound of my voice . . . Either way . . . you find
that you're becoming more and more sleepy . . . more and more tired
. . . more and more relaxed . . . Feeling better . . . and better . . . with
every breath that you take . . . With every breath that you take . . . you
are becoming more peaceful . . . more relaxed . . . feeling better . . .
than you have before . . . So now just allow yourself to go to sleep . . .
this very moment . . . Sleep . . . sleep . . . go into a deep . . . sound
. . . sleep . . . and you will stay in this sound sleep even after my voice
goes away . . . and allows you . . . to sleep quietly . . . to sleep soundly
. . . So now just sleep . . . sleep . . . sleep.

Reducing Stress

Virtually any hypnosis session will assist in reducing stress,
regardless of the topic. It is a natural byproduct of relaxation. However, there are many times where it is advantageous to dedicate an entire session to stress reduction.

Stress Reduction Script

The following session is completely self-contained
and does not need to be inserted into any of the templates. Simply read the entire session onto your recording
device, or read it to yourself depending on how you want
to proceed.

Take a deep breath . . . and hold it for a few seconds . . . exhale
and relax . . . Now take a second deep breath, as deep as you can . . .

and as you exhale just allow any stress to let go . . . Take a third deep breath . . . as deep as you can . . . hold it . . . and exhale . . . just think to yourself the words "relax now."

This is your new solution for stress . . . Whenever you become stressed in the future . . . you'll simply relax . . . take three deep breaths . . . and on your third one, as you exhale . . . you will simply say to yourself the words *relax now.*

You are now developing a new way to relax . . . you are letting go of the stress of the past . . . You wish to no longer have depression or anger in your life . . . From now on you choose to be relaxed . . . You choose to be calm . . . and you choose to be in control in all that you do . . . because your health is important to you . . . You are changing the way that you used to act and you are replacing it with the new, positive suggestions I am about to give you . . .

By following these few simple suggestions . . . you'll find yourself being stress free in all that you do . . . You'll find yourself being relaxed in situations that you may not have been relaxed in before . . . and with your new relaxed lifestyle . . . you'll find yourself being happier . . . more positive minded . . . and enjoying all that you do.

The first suggestion is that whenever you find yourself having negative, unproductive thoughts, you'll immediately say to yourself the word *STOP!* . . . Let me repeat that to you so it is perfectly clear . . . Whenever you find yourself having negative, unproductive thoughts, you'll immediately say to yourself the word *STOP!* . . . and as soon as you say the word *STOP!* . . . you'll find that the negative thoughts you were having just disappear . . . It will give you the opportunity to start a new, positive thought process.

The next technique is the art of acceptance . . . accepting things as they are . . . rather than allowing them to escalate out of control . . . From this moment on . . . anytime you find yourself getting stressed, because of a situation that seems to be going out of control . . . You will stop worrying about what could happen . . . all the negative scenarios . . . and instead . . . you will accept . . . what has happened for exactly what it is . . . You can use your thought process to think the situation through to see what reasonable outcomes may be there . . . realizing that once you have worked them through, they are always better than if you let your mind run free and worry . . . Worry is a thing of the past . . . it is now replaced . . . with relaxation.

You are now in control . . . of your thoughts . . . your feelings . . . and your emotions . . . you have become an actor . . . rather than a reactor . . . which simply means that in any given situation . . . you . . . and only you . . . choose . . . how you are going to react . . . or to act . . . and now you choose to act . . . calmly . . . positively . . . and in control.

Just for a moment I would like you to concentrate on your breathing . . . take a breath in . . . and exhale, and as soon as you feel all the breath leave your body and you are prepared to take another breath, count to yourself quietly, twenty-five . . . take a second breath, not necessarily a deep breath, just a normal one, and exhale . . . and when that breath is finished count to yourself, twenty-four . . . then take another normal breath, whatever length seems comfortable to you . . . and exhale . . . then count to yourself, twenty-three . . . and continue doing this on your own, with another breath, counting twenty-two, and twenty-one, all the way down to one . . . and as soon as you take your last deep breath, exhale, and say the number one, you will open your eyes . . . feeling calm . . . and relaxed . . . in every way . . . in fact, you will find yourself more relaxed than you have ever been before.

So continue counting even as I speak . . . each one of your breaths . . . concentrating on your breathing . . . noticing the flow of the air . . . as it enters your body . . . fills you up . . . and then leaves once again . . . study the sensations you feel . . . with every breath you take you relax more and more, with every breath you take you feel more peaceful and more serene as you go down deeper and deeper into the relaxed state . . . and as soon as you count to the number one, you will open your eyes once again feeling wonderful in every way.

Hypnosis Birthing

Natural forms of hypnosis childbirth have become very popular in recent years. Many birthing mothers and couples are becoming aware of natural forms of pain management and hypnosis relaxation as a way to eliminate the need for anesthesia that in many cases can hinder the enjoyment of such a beautiful experience.

Fear and Expectation

Fear and anxiety cause the body to tense up. This tensing of the body during childbirth can cause many difficulties and is often one of the major causes of pain and discomfort. It is important to be able to relax and let go completely during the procedure so as to allow the natural process to flow freely.

It is important to realize that fear and anxiety are subjective and not objective. This means that you cannot hold them or display them in any way. They are in your head. Although they may seem very real to you, in fact, they are not real at all. They are expectations of future events. If you are afraid that there will be pain and discomfort coming up very shortly, this will create anxiety in you that will cause you to tense up and in turn display the pain that you expected. Keep in mind that your subconscious mind will give you exactly what you ask for, and if you are focusing on pain, you will receive it.

Alert!

It is extremely important before attempting to utilize hypnosis or any other natural relaxation or pain reduction technique to check with a proper medical professional to ensure that these techniques are appropriate for you. Just as every birthing mother is different, so too are people's reactions and levels of success with hypnosis.

In order to eliminate fear and anxiety, realize that they do not exist in the present. They only exist in the past and in the future. At this very moment everything is okay and stress free. This very moment, all that is important for you is right now. Think about how you are feeling right at this very moment. You are fine and it is okay to feel the way you are feeling right now. This is the best that life has to give you at this moment.

Chapter 11 has a script that will help you through the birthing process by teaching you how to focus on the now, even while you are in a situation where you think you may be worried. It is a breathing exercise that will help you let go of future expectations as well as negativity that you may have had from the past.

Healing from Within

We have just barely begun to scratch the surface of understanding the powers of the subconscious mind. It is truly a marvelous thing. What the mind can conceive the mind can achieve. This applies especially in the area of healing. The subconscious mind has the ability to heal the majority of afflictions that affect the body.

The Subconscious Knows All

The subconscious mind is responsible for keeping everything within your body in running order and in control. Whether you are wide awake or sleeping, your subconscious mind is always working, seeing to it that your heart is always beating and that your lungs are working properly and breathing. It is the part of your mind that makes sure that blood is pumping to your entire system, that your skin stays healthy. It is even responsible for the growth of your fingernails and is responsible for regulating your body temperature. Every function of your body is controlled by the subconscious mind.

Just think for a moment about the growth of the fetus. The subconscious mind is responsible for the entire development of the baby. It helps the baby grow within the womb at each and every different stage. It is the part of the mind that decides when the baby's different organs will be formed, the part that tells it when the fingers and toes will be formed. Everything is known within the subconscious mind. It provides the blueprint for this newborn's life. These blueprints stay within each and every one of us for our entire life.

 Fact

> When trying to heal an affliction or reduce pain, it is important not to label what it is that you have. Labeling encourages ownership. Rather than stating you have this specific sickness, simply call it a disorder, dysfunction, or temporary inconvenience. It is much easier to eliminate something when it is not your own.

Remember that it is natural for you to be healthy and happy. It is unnatural for you to have sickness and misery. Your blueprints from when you were born, that developed you from a single cell, brought you all the way from conception to a happy and healthy child. Those blueprints still remain within your subconscious mind, even as you grow older. They help you stay healthy and correct problems as they arise.

Healing Process

It is difficult to create a generic healing script because there are many things that might require healing. A script can be created for virtually anything that needs to be healed. The theater of the mind script in Chapter 4 can be used for most healing topics. Simply insert what it is you want to heal or improve in wherever the script mentions your "goal." It is important while you are using this script or any other that you use your imagination and imagine yourself as the end result. Imagine yourself as already having been healed. Use as much detail in the visualization as possible. The more visual and the more emotion you can use in this process the better.

Daydream Your Way to Health

Another technique to eliminate pain or create healing is the use of daydreaming. Daydreaming is a very powerful tool when used creatively. The daydream state is actually in what is known as the theta brain wave state. Daydreaming is also a form of self-hypnosis. When you daydream you are using your imagination.

 Essential

Keep in mind that even though you may feel better after just one session, you must continue the process for the entire twenty-one days to create a new habit of health. Stopping for just one day can eliminate all progress.

The subconscious mind does not understand the difference between a real memory and an imagined memory. So when you daydream, imagine yourself as the healthy person that you wish to be. Imagine yourself without the disorder, as having risen above it and conquered it. One of the reasons that daydreaming is so powerful is that it involves feelings and is very visual.

Chapter 10
Business and Success

The following scripts for business accomplishments and personal success are to be used within the templates found at the end of Chapter 5. You have a choice of two separate templates, one for an analytical session and one for a non-analytical session. Use the suggestibility tests at the end of Chapter 3 to determine which of the two templates will work best for you.

Arrive at Appointments on Time

There are many reasons why people who are chronically late to appointments are the way they are. Whether it's time management problems or a lack of motivation, to those who are waiting for you to show up for the appointment, it displays a lack of interest or respect in what they are offering. Being on time for appointments positively affects the way people look at you and enhances your self-image.

 Essential

> The actual length of a script is not important. It can be just as effective whether it is two sentences or two pages long. The purpose of the script is simply what you would say to the subconscious mind to correct a problem once you have its receptive and undivided attention.

You have decided that now is the time to take control of your life . . . to meet your engagements each and every day on time . . . and the way you are going to be on time from now on . . . is by changing some of your past negative behaviors . . . into new positive behaviors . . . You are going to be on time for all appointments, engagements, and functions because you want to be . . . The first step in being on time to appointments is to change your thinking toward them . . . From now on you will give a new importance to your appointments . . . You feel an urgency to get there on time . . . In fact, you feel they are so important to you that you want to get to your appointments early . . . You'll always plan from this moment forward to arrive at your scheduled appointments a minimum of fifteen minutes early, and even earlier than that if time permits . . . By doing this you will find that you will arrive at your appointments on time, even if unexpected things occur on the way, such as bad traffic or any other hindrance . . . by leaving early you will still have time to spare . . . You do not have to worry about wasting time because you realize that if you arrive at an appointment early you can put the additional time to good use . . . One way to do that would be to bring a book that you have been wanting to read with you . . . or maybe some paperwork or a notebook with you so that if you have additional time you can make plans or accomplish other tasks . . . From now on you give importance to all your appointments . . . You are professional in your thinking and arrive early . . . By doing so, others will see you as a professional . . . They will see you as a successful, courteous person . . . Showing up to an appointment on time, or especially early, shows that you are courteous and care about the appointment that you have . . . People will respect you more . . . People will appreciate you more . . . You will feel more confident that you are in control of your time . . . From this moment forward you manage your time successfully.

Enhance Creativity

This script is designed to expand your creativity and to enhance what you already have. It is created in two different formats. The first portion should be read onto your recording device so that you may listen to it just as you would any other session. The last paragraph is designed more as an autosuggestion script. When reading this script onto your recording device, pause wherever you see the three consecutive dots long enough to repeat that segment to yourself quietly.

You are a creative person and you will find that each day your creativity will grow more and more. Your mind is much more open and you can easily reach into your subconscious to increase your creativity.

You are constantly open to new ideas and new concepts. You look at everything with a positive attitude, being open-minded. Because you are open-minded, you learn more each and every day. Every day that goes by you have more knowledge than the day before. Ideas flow freely through your mind, and many times you need to stop to take notes because you have so many new and interesting ideas.

You are becoming more and more creative each and every day. You have the ability to retrieve creative ideas and knowledge from your subconscious mind on a constant basis that you have not been able to retrieve before. You are truly becoming the person that you wish to become.

As you hear the following suggestions, repeat them to yourself quietly.

I am constantly improving each and every day . . . I am creative . . . I am creating a better and more improved me . . . Once I have decided the traits and abilities I would like to have . . . I create those abilities in myself . . . I am creative . . . I allow myself to become that person . . . that person that I know I can be . . . I have no limitations . . . I can create, do, or be anything I can imagine . . . I always think outside the box . . . my mind is open to all possibilities . . . I am creative . . . and my creativity is always improving.

Become a Money Magnet

The purpose of this script is to prepare you to accept financial success as it is presented to you. Many people, even when given the opportunity, are not aware that it is happening or capable of receiving it. This script will help you believe in yourself as well as be a receptive vessel in attracting money.

You believe in the power of your subconscious mind to cause you to succeed. What the mind can conceive, the mind can achieve. You believe in yourself. You believe in your success. You expect success . . . There is no time limit to success. You can be successful now or later . . . but you choose to be successful NOW!

NOW is the time . . . Now is your time . . . So give yourself the okay . . . Give yourself the permission . . . right NOW . . . to be successful . . . You deserve prosperity . . . You expect prosperity . . . Prosperity, health, and happiness are natural. Meagerness, sickness, and sadness are unnatural. You have a right to be happy, to be natural, to be successful, and to have plenty of money.

You are a money magnet . . . Money, success, and opportunities seem to be drawn to you constantly . . . They find you wherever you are . . . You are now aware of opportunities around you and are able to take advantage of them . . . You are successful. Money is always circulating in your life. You release it with joy, and it returns to you multiplied in a wonderful way . . . Money flows to you in abundance. You use it for good purposes and are grateful for the riches of your mind.

You are a money magnet . . . You are always on the lookout for good, positive opportunities. New opportunities easily and frequently come your way . . . You are on top of your game and recognize all opportunities as they occur . . . You always seem to be at the right place at the right time . . . Change your thoughts and you change your destiny. You are a money magnet.

Gain a Positive Mental Attitude

It is important to be open-minded in listening to this script. Approach it with an attitude of optimism, desire, and expectancy. Remember that while virtually anyone can be hypnotized, anyone can also resist it. Be conscious of your resistance and let down your walls for success.

You are changing your way of thinking and becoming a more positive person because you want to. When someone asks you how you are, you will say, "Wonderful." You know that if you think you are wonderful, then you are wonderful. You are able to replace every negative thought with one that is positive. You feel empowered with this new ability. You use words that describe the positive power and energy, words like happy . . . thoughtful . . . peaceful . . . loving . . . kind . . . gracious . . . independent . . . helpful . . . gracious . . . honest . . . dependable . . . intelligent . . . resilient . . . (add any other positive words that are appropriate) . . . You see yourself as a person who has the ability to change a negative thought into a positive thought, without hesitation.

Positive feelings increase health, happiness, and strength. Being positive helps you to look at the world in a different light. You are now positive in all things. You want to be positive . . . Things seem to go your way more often . . . and you attract positive to you when you are being positive. Positive people like to be around other positive people, helping you to attract what you really want in your life.

Being positive helps you to see the good side of things . . . The glass is half full rather than half empty. All events, whether favorable or not, have a positive side to them and therefore are easier to deal with.

You find the positive in all people you deal with. Everyone has positive qualities in them . . . You now take the time to find them . . . You now take the time to list the things in your life that you are thankful for. Take the time to list them one by one and you will find that you have much to be positive for.

Rather than dwelling on what you cannot do or what you do not want . . . you now only dwell on what you can do and what you do want . . . You are positive in all that you do.

Overcome Procrastination

One of the most difficult things to accomplish for those who are afflicted with procrastination is to finally decide to take action and do something about it. A word of warning: do not to listen to this script in the late evening hours. You may just find yourself up until three or four in the morning doing your spring cleaning and other long neglected tasks.

You are now happy and delighted whenever you think of the things that you would like or need to accomplish. It feels good to have a purpose to direct your energies toward each day. By completing all of your busy tasks now, your free time becomes truly that: your free time. If there is work to do, it feels good to do it and to complete it. Any assignments, homework, or household tasks or chores are actually fun to do and complete. When you are at work or school, you feel calm and relaxed about anything added to your list that will require your time and attention later in the day, week, or even year, because you now have a strong sense of motivation and purpose. You even feel peaceful about doing these tasks and completing all that is required to be successful at work, school, or even at home.

Now when there is an assignment or project, you get it done at the earliest time possible, knowing that this way you can also find time to do other things you value and enjoy. You simply do what needs to be done . . . and move on . . . with ease and enjoyment during the whole process.

It feels so good to complete things that you wonder why you waited so long in the past to get to them . . . and you feel great about yourself and your life . . . as you should . . . because you deserve to feel good about yourself, and now you are doing the things that reflect that good feeling more and more often.

Your new motto in life is "do it now," and that is exactly what you do. You now look at all of your chores, tasks, and other things to be done as challenges, and you now approach those challenges with excitement and a positive attitude.

Each day create a Do list. On this list you write down all of the challenges that you are faced with on that day. In the evening you can check this list to see how many of these challenges you have met and completed. You can then enter new challenges that need to be accomplished for the coming day. This way you will be organized in your activities and confident now that procrastination is in the past.

Excel at Public Speaking

Public speaking phobias are quite common and can manifest as simply having the jitters before a presentation to being violently ill. Fear of failure is a very prevalent concern among speakers. In addition to listening to this session in the privacy of your own home, listen to it just before the big presentation is to occur.

You are interesting and you have a lot of important things to say. You are a brilliant and accomplished expert in your field. People come to listen to you because they are interested in what you have to say.

You are a great speaker. You are interesting and provide information these people have never heard before. You will allow yourself to speak with an interesting and intelligent flow that will keep everyone invested and interested in your topic because you are an interesting and intelligent speaker.

You are highly organized. You have done your homework and research for this presentation. Your notes are in your hands. You feel very confident. If you need them, you can comfortably glance down at them . . . completely relaxed . . . a natural movement.

You are prepared. You are polished . . . neatly dressed . . . professional . . . ready to impress your audience with your poise . . . ease . . . and, clearly, your expertise on the subject. You know you are good at what you do. You know this material. You are focused . . . all the material is there in your subconscious. With every sentence, you become more self-assured . . . pausing . . . breathing . . . periodically scanning the audience, occasionally making eye contact . . . all the time in your relaxed place . . . in your relaxed state.

You are so confident of your belief in your presentation that you know you are helping your audience. At the end of your presentation you know you will receive thunderous applause because of the fine presentation that you delivered. You are the ultimate public speaker!

Motivate Yourself for Success

The basic principle of the law of attraction is that whatever you place your thoughts, focus, and attention on, you draw to you. The basis of this session is to be positive and success minded so as to attract success and opportunity to you.

You are thankful for your success . . . You are positive minded . . . You affect all those around you in positive ways . . . You are happy . . . You smile often . . . Each morning you begin your day peacefully, happily, and with a smile . . . You greet people with a smile, enthusiasm, and interest . . . You encourage and inspire others. You are successful.

You are positive at all times, and in control . . . You think good thoughts . . . You fill your mind with only good thoughts and good feelings . . . helping you to feel happy . . . You realize that things are as they are . . . You accept things as they come . . . You practice awareness . . . being open to your surroundings . . . and are aware of opportunities as they arise. You are successful.

You welcome success with joy, happiness, and open arms . . . Things are going your way . . . success has a way of finding you . . . You attract positive people and success to yourself . . . You enjoy and are comfortable being around positive, successful people . . .

You network as often as possible with successful people . . . You are a success magnet that keeps attracting goodness and abundance to you. You are successful.

You now act and think as someone who already is successful . . . Positive opportunities come to you . . . You deserve to be successful . . . it is your divine right to be successful . . . You have earned it and now is your time . . . It is okay to be successful . . . You are prepared for success . . . and success is attracted to you . . . Good times are here . . . You are physically, emotionally, and financially secure . . . You walk with your head held high, proud of your success, which is reflected to others by your actions. You are successful.

It is natural for you to feel good . . . It is natural for you to be healthy and strong . . . You feel terrific . . . physically . . . and mentally fit . . . Your mind is keen and creative . . . Your memory continually improves and is open to new experiences . . . You are successful.

Help Thinking Big

The basic nature of the conscious mind is to remain the same. It is a creature of habit that does not like to stretch to do anything different than it always has done. It will fight to remain in its comfort zone. It is important to be aware of this constant resistance that you may experience as you are in the process of exceeding your programming by thinking big. Rest assured that perseverance will pay off. Once you have created a new habit of thinking big in all that you do, it will become much easier to do since the conscious mind will then accept it.

You think big in all that you do. In setting your personal and business goals you reach for the sky. You realize that if you do not stretch, you cannot grow, therefore you stretch and reach for more with each and every decision you make. In order to grow you must step out of your comfort zone. You must do something different than you are currently doing. You think big.

You go for the gold. In all that you do you have a winning attitude. Rather than being competitive you are creative. The only person that you need to compete with is yourself. You are always trying to be your best. You give 100 percent in all that you do. And you do it with a smile. Remember if you shoot for the sun you may just get it, but if you don't you can still reach the moon. So there is no downside . . . it is a win-win situation. You think big.

In anything that you do you take a moment to think if there is a way you can supersize it. You think about how you can make anything you do better. How can it be fantastic?

In every area of your life you reach for more. In your work, goals, relationships, personal life, and even recreation, you make it spectacular. By thinking big in all that you do, not only will you obtain greater success, but more opportunity will come your way. You think big.

You know that you are the best you that you can be. No one else has your abilities in quite the way that you do. You put a different, unique twist on everything that you do. You think big.

Adopt a Winning Attitude

This is a topic that will help you in every area of your life, from business and finances to relationships and health. A winning attitude will not only help you but will also draw other like-minded people to you. There is really no downside to this; the sky's the limit.

From this point on, the only thoughts that you will have are positive thoughts. You will rid your mind of negative words like *can't*, *won't*, *should have*, *would have*, *and could have*. From now on, your mind will only think in terms of "I can" and "I will." You are a winner!

You truly feel that the world is out to help you. Opportunities open up to you at every turn. You are a winner. You believe that only positive things happen to you and that everything happens for a reason. You know that you are a piece that fits into a wonderful puzzle, and you are so happy to be part of it all. You know the future is full of many exciting and amazing moments just waiting to happen. Your hopefulness fills every room you enter and makes others around you energized and renewed.

You are an impressively strong person with an unwavering view of yourself. You are a confident and energetic person regardless of the circumstances. You are proud of who you are. You are as solidly rooted as a giant, ancient oak tree . . . never will you fall or sway. You are a winner.

You do not know what the future holds, but you are certain that you will be prepared and persevere through anything. Being a survivor is natural to you. Others marvel at your calmness regardless of the situation. You thrive on the uncertainty of the future . . . each day you are becoming more and more confident. You are a winner.

Chapter 11
Health Issues

The following scripts are for various health-related issues. One of the scripts includes the imagining of a healing white light. While utilizing any of these scripts, it is important to use your imagination in as much detail as possible and imagine yourself as being the already successful you. In addition to imagining, it is important to have as many emotions involved in the process as possible.

Energy Boost

The following energy boost script utilizes your imagination to create energy in any situation that you may need. Take time to practice imagining and listen to the script before the event that requires the energy boost.

 Alert!

Before dealing with any of the following healing techniques, it is important to check with a doctor to ensure that medical treatment is not required. These hypnosis sessions are designed as a helpmate and not a replacement for proper medical care.

You are strong and full of confidence. You feel better than you ever felt before. You feel young and fresh. You are full of energy and happiness. You want to try new things. You want to prove to the world that you can do it. As you already know you can.

Whenever you are in need of an energy boost you will follow these steps . . .

First you will focus on your posture. Take note of how you are standing. The first step in receiving your energy boost is to stand tall with your shoulders back, chest out, and head up straight. Your posture should reflect one of pride and enthusiasm.

It is very important that you like doing this and you put a smile on your face throughout the entire procedure. It is a proven fact that happiness brings you energy, whereas sadness drains you of energy. Since the subconscious mind gives the same importance to imagination as reality, even if you do not feel happy at the moment, still put a smile on your face. This is an important factor in convincing your subconscious that you are ready for your energy boost.

Take three deep breaths and with each breath you take in imagine yourself breathing in pure energy from the universe. As you exhale, imagine yourself releasing any negativity or doubt.

As you are doing this you will feel the energy begin to surge within you. Take a moment right now to imagine this scenario. Imagine yourself right now in a situation where you would require an energy boost. Imagine yourself standing tall with your chest out, shoulders back, and head up straight. Imagine yourself with a big smile and a look of confidence on your face. Now take a deep breath and imagine yourself breathing in pure energy, and as you exhale release any negativity or doubt. Take a second deep breath, once again breathing in pure energy and exhaling any negativity or doubt, and on your third deep breath breathe in as much energy as you can and hold it for three seconds, and then release it, letting go of the last of any negativity or doubt.

You now have confidence that you can achieve anything that you desire. You are happy and confident and feel good about yourself. You are a winner.

Choose to Be Healthy

Everything begins with a choice. You make a choice to be active, and you make a choice to be inactive. The following scripts will help you along your path to being healthy; however, they also require you to make a choice.

You have come to this point in your life where you have decided to be healthy. For whatever reason, you realize that now you must make a conscious choice to change the way you have been living or maybe even thinking and replace it with positive actions.

Your past is behind you. Keep in mind that each and every breath you take is a brand new one. This very breath you are taking right now has never been taken before. It is completely unique from the last one. You have control over each new breath, whether you make it a long breath or a short one. You even have the control to hold your breath. Just as each new breath is not like the one before and can be changed at a moment's notice, so can you control the future of your health.

Being healthy is a matter of choice. You must choose to be healthy. And in order to do that you must be constantly vigilant in whatever suggestions you allow your mind to accept. Everything in life starts with a thought. If someone were to tell you all day long that you looked sick, you would eventually begin to feel sick if you allowed yourself to accept those suggestions. Even though that may not happen, your subconscious mind is constantly being challenged by suggestions that can cause you to be unhealthy. Suggestions come through the television and radio on a daily basis from pharmaceutical ads suggesting that you may be sick.

You hear suggestions by friends, coworkers, classmates, family, in the supermarket, and virtually anywhere you go. You even give yourself many suggestions on a daily basis that may not be healthy.

From this point forward you will practice thought stopping. At any time that you may hear a negative suggestion about the way you look, feel, act, or anything about your health, you immediately eliminate that suggestion by saying out loud the word *cancel* and then replacing it with a positive thought.

Any time that you find yourself saying a negative statement, you will immediately end it in a positive manner, and if you cannot find a positive way to end it, you will simply not finish it at all.

You now screen your thoughts. You think positive thoughts of yourself, always thinking of yourself as a healthy person. Even if you are not healthy presently, you will now think of yourself as healthy. You imagine yourself as healthy. You act as if you are a healthy person.

Take a moment right now and imagine yourself as if you are standing right in front of yourself as a healthy person. Imagine yourself as the goal you. See yourself in as much detail as possible with a big smile on your face, feeling wonderful. This image you are imagining of yourself right now is you. Be that person. Congratulations on your new, healthy life.

Eating Healthy

Everywhere you look today there are programs, books, television shows, and even celebrities telling you how you should eat healthy. Grocery stores and pharmacies have entire shelves designated solely for diet and weight-loss programs. Keep in mind, whatever you decide to do, that it is something that you can stick with fairly easily. Eating healthy is a lifelong event.

From this moment forward you eat healthy. You find yourself each and every day having more of a desire to be healthy. Adding healthy foods to your life will give you more energy and help you to feel much better. Each day you are looking for new, healthier ways to eat, replacing any unhealthy habits with healthy ones that you will enjoy.

You find that now you eat much slower than before. You take time to notice each bite of food and chew it thoroughly before taking the next one. By eating slowly you will notice that you are filling up quicker even though you are eating less food. You now notice that you may not even be able to finish the food that you have placed on your plate. It makes you proud that you can eat in this new, healthy manner.

Rich, greasy, sugary, and fattening foods no longer appeal to you, as life-giving, healthy foods taste better than ever before. Let me repeat that one more time: rich, greasy, sugary, and fattening foods no longer appeal to you, as life-giving, healthy foods taste better than ever before.

You now find yourself drinking more water than you have in the past. That wonderful water will be your ally in helping you to be and remain healthy. You find yourself enjoying water more and more each day, that wonderful, clear, refreshing water tastes better than ever before and will truly quench your thirst. Drinking water, especially before each meal, will fill you up so you will not eat as much as before. Water also helps to flush out your system quicker and helps your entire body to function properly. It is the proper lubrication that the body is in need of. From now on you give your body what it needs and are refreshed by it.

You'll find that by eating healthier you will have much more energy than ever before. You will have energy that can be put to good use, and you will find yourself being more energetic. You will find yourself doing more so you can use this energy, which will also help you to attain the body that you wish to attain.

Healing Faster

One of the best helpmates of healing faster is relaxation. The more that you can relax, the easier and quicker your body can heal. Things that can hinder the healing process are anxiety and stress. Hypnosis helps to alleviate and deal with both.

A healthy body means a healthy mind. You are calm and relaxed. You are focusing your mind on positive thoughts. Imagine yourself full of health and vitality, just the way you want to be, and keep this image focused in your mind as you direct your awareness to your health. Feel and imagine a new healthy you.

You are becoming so much calmer, so much more relaxed than ever before. Your whole outlook on life is improving and you begin to take each day as it comes in a positive manner. You feel a sense of acceptance, a feeling of peace and serenity deep within you. Your breathing becomes more natural and your entire nervous system begins to function more efficiently. Your entire body is working in peace and harmony together.

Your body heals faster by the day, faster by the hour, because this is something that you want. You are the master of your mind and you are now willing your body to heal faster. What your mind can conceive, it can achieve. The rate that your body can heal is entirely up to you. Your breathing becomes normal and your entire body becomes more balanced and stable. You are calm and relaxed.

Healing White Light

A wonderful visual technique you can use is the healing white light. Imagine a healing white light just above your head. This is a light that heals completely or relieves you from all your pain. The light will act similarly to a scanner from a photocopier. As the light descends over your head, scanning your face and on down, the pain will recede from everywhere the light goes. You will feel wonderful. You then continue to scan lower and lower and scan your entire body, and all the pain is gone.

 Essential

You can also imagine that you are filled with a healing white light. As you make a survey of your entire body, see if you can find where there might be leaks and the light is escaping. Those areas need to be healed, and you should mentally imagine yourself fixing those leaks. Plug them up so the light is contained within you. Fixing these leaks will lessen your pain.

I want you to use your imagination. Take a deep breath and hold it for a second; as you breathe in imagine yourself breathing in pure energy from the universe. You can even visualize this energy as being a bright, white, healing, fluffy substance. Each time you exhale you release negativity and discomfort. Each time you inhale you inhale more of that pure white energy until it fills you up completely. Imagine the energy goes in and remains with you until you are completely filled. Now make a mental scan over your entire body to see if you have any energy leaks. As you do, if you see any leaks you will see the white, comfortable energy visibly escaping. If you see any of these leaks, use your imagination and imagine yourself repairing them. Just imagine it and it will happen, until they are all repaired (pause a few moments).

Now that you have completely repaired any leaks, you can allow the energy to continue to flow through you. As you inhale and exhale, the energy both enters and can flow outwards, continually keeping you energized and feeling wonderful. As you continue to imagine this energy flowing in and out of you and filling you up, it seems to absorb itself into every cell of your being. It fills you up so much that it seems to form a protective shield around your body. This protective shield protects you from any negativity. No longer can the influence of anyone or anything drain your energy away.

Hypnosis Birthing—Relaxation

Being relaxed is key to having a wonderful birthing experience. This exercise will help you eliminate negativity so you can allow yourself to relax and help everything run smoothly and enjoyably.

See yourself breathing easily . . . completely relaxed. You are about to give birth to your child . . . This is a wonderful event in your life and you have been waiting many months for this moment to occur.

You feel comfortable, relaxed, and pain free because the pain in childbirth comes from fear, tension, and anxiety. You do not have fear, tension, or anxiety about childbirth because you are thinking in the now. Those negative feelings only exist in the past due to the things others talk about and in the future due to unfounded anticipation. Everything right now is fine and there is only relaxation. Negative feelings of fear do not exist now. You will not experience any pain before, during, or after the birth of your child because you are in control and this is what you want.

You let everything go as if you are detached from your body and allow yourself to relax, leaving enough awareness in your body to respond to the requests of the doctor should he have instructions for you.

You will be able to observe your child being born as if you were an observer watching the scene from the seats in a movie theater, feeling no discomfort or pain until the entire procedure is over. You will be able to enjoy the entire birth. You will feel the excitement and joy of this wondrous event in a relaxed, controlled environment.

Hypnosis Birthing—Breathing

The following script will help you breathe properly throughout your childbearing process. Breathing is very important to your overall success as it will help you relax and also give you a focal point. Take the time to practice this session as often as you can so you can be proficient with it before your actual birthing procedure.

You have a desire to use self-hypnosis and special breathing techniques that can help to bring about a shorter, easier, and more joyful birthing experience, free of harmful drugs for you and your baby. You will bring your child into this world in a more comfortable manner, awake, alert, and fully in control. Even your recuperation period will be so much quicker and easier. You have made a very wise decision, one that will give you and your new child a head start in life.

You are now receiving the tools you need to help you to be relaxed and calm through the birthing process. Through this knowledge you are able to take away the unknown so as to remove any fear and anticipation. Through relaxation you will learn how to work with your body's natural rhythm instead of fighting it. One of the main keys of being in control is knowledge, and you have taken the time to prepare and understand the stages of the birthing process and how deep-relaxation techniques can help you.

Realize right now that you are not in a deep trance state or a state of unawareness, instead you are in a daydreaming state, as if you were watching yourself on a movie screen. You can continue to imagine yourself as if you were sitting in a theater watching yourself on the screen throughout the entire process. If at any time you find yourself becoming stressed or experiencing any discomfort that you do not wish to, simply remind yourself that you are sitting in this theater watching yourself on the screen and will not experience any discomfort or inconvenience. This way you do not experience anything directly.

You are completely aware of what is going on around you even though you are focused on being totally relaxed. You focus simply on the now, realizing that what has happened and what has not yet happened is irrelevant. All that matters is what is going on right now, and right now you are totally relaxed and completely in control. By being in the now you have eliminated stress and anxiety, as they both exist only in the future and the past. Having eliminated them, you will find that your body can stay relaxed since they are the reason your body tends to contract and tighten, which is what causes pain and hinders the birthing process. You are relaxed.

Once you have begun the birthing process, you will focus on your breathing. Even though you are focusing on your breathing, you will still be able to hear everything else going on around you. Therefore, if you are given a task to do or asked a question by whomever is conducting the birthing process, you will be able to respond easily and immediately even though you are focusing on your breathing.

You will now be guided through the process of how focusing on your breathing should be done. Right now I would like you to take a slow, deep breath . . . and once you have exhaled completely . . . mentally say to yourself the number . . . one. Take a second deep breath and upon totally completing that one . . . say to yourself the number . . . two. Continue counting after each breath until you get to twelve breaths and then begin the process over again counting from one to twelve.

You will continue doing this until you are given instructions to stop. If at any time you lose your place or count more than the number twelve, simply start over again at one. Continue now to count your breaths on your own until you hear my voice again.

(Insert enough time to count four to five cycles of twelve, then conduct the awakening.)

Relieve Migraines

This session is designed to help relieve or eliminate migraine headaches. Once again, it is important before using this script, especially if you suffer from chronic migraines, to check with a medical professional to ensure that your migraines are not signifying a serious medical condition.

I would like you to think about the inconvenience you are feeling right now and imagine it as an object . . . It can be a football or a baseball or even a Frisbee . . . I want you to take that object and throw it away . . . releasing you from all the pain . . . just watch it sail out of sight and out of your life. You do not need the inconvenience of a headache . . . Any time you feel a headache coming on, you release it in the same manner.

Another thing you will do in the future as a signal or an immediate release cue is to place your fingertips on the back of your neck and gently apply pressure . . . feeling the tension melt away . . . When you begin to feel this type of inconvenience come on . . . apply gentle pressure and you will feel yourself immediately relaxing. You will take a deep breath, relaxing the muscles and pressure, making it not able to materialize.

Relax and shape and form the headache and throw it away. As you relax you do not need the headache. Anytime you feel a headache coming on, you release it. Place the tips of your fingers on the back of your neck and apply a very gentle pressure and the tension goes away.

My Special Place—an Escape

The following script will help you create a location within your mind that you can escape to anytime you wish. It is a wonderful place to be used for meditation, contemplation, reflection, and even prayer. It is a spot to escape to or simply to enjoy a quick break.

I'd like you to use your imagination right now. Let your imagination roam free and allow the first thought that comes into your head to take hold and develop. Just imagine that you are in an empty space and you are going to create a beautiful, relaxing, peaceful room. This will be a room that you can resort to any time you like.

I would like you to create the most comfortable piece of furniture that you can imagine. Just create the most comfortable piece of furniture that you can think of, whether it's a very plush recliner or an overstuffed feather bed. Create it in your mind right now, see all the details of it, the color, the texture. See it as clearly in your mind as possible. Now imagine yourself sitting or lying on this piece of furniture as we continue our task.

Let's begin with the walls of this room. Imagine how big or small you would like the room to be. What are the walls made of? The only limitation you have is that of your own imagination. So imagine the walls. Are they painted? . . . Are they made out of cement or plaster? . . . Are they wooden or glass? . . . Now I would like you to take a moment and imagine what you would like to have for a floor. What is the floor made of? Is it made of wood, cement, tiles, linoleum, sand, or maybe even grass? . . . Make it out of whatever you would like . . . It can also be whatever color you would like. Just see it clearly in your mind's eye . . .

Now how about the ceiling? What is the ceiling made of? You can make it as fancy or as simple as you like . . . You can even put in recessed lighting, or even a chandelier if you care to . . . Create the ceiling now and make it look however you would like it to.

You have now created the complete parameters of your room. Before we continue, look around now and see if there is anything else you would like to add, such as windows, doors, skylights, or any other permanent fixtures. Take a moment to finish any of these tasks.

What other kind of furniture would you like to create in this room that would help it to be a very relaxing, comfortable place for you to be in? Go ahead and create now any other pieces of large furniture that you would like, maybe a bureau, or tables, a desk, vanity, maybe even an easel so you can do some art work . . . Take your time and be creative . . .

Now create any smaller furnishings you would like to have in this room. You may want to create some lamps, knickknacks, books, maybe a small bookshelf . . . Create everything down to the smallest detail, even picture frames, figurines, and personal items. Take a few moments now to create all the little things that will make this room comfortable and personal to you.

Look around at everything you have created in this room and commit it to memory. You can change this room anytime you like. You can add items, remove items, or even change the main features of the room if it suits your liking.

Any time in the future that you want to come back to this room you can do so. All you need to do to come back is to take a deep breath and simply say to yourself, "relax now." Upon saying "relax now" you can allow yourself to return to this room.

Chapter 12
Family and Relationship Issues

The scripts in this chapter are designed for various topics that can be used within your family or for enjoyment. Most of the scripts are based on focusing and using your imagination. When conducting scripts or using these techniques on your children, especially in the first three topics, take the time to explain to them how important their imagination is in achieving their goals.

Bedwetting

There are several factors that may contribute to bedwetting. First, the subject may be sleeping too deeply and not wake up in time. Second, the subject is drinking too many liquids prior to going to sleep. There may also be an underlying medical problem, so if bedwetting continues even after utilizing these scripts, it may be a good idea to check with your medical professional.

Every night when you go to bed you feel confident that you are now successful in going to bed without wetting. You no longer sleep if you feel the urge to go to the bathroom. That is part of your past, from this moment it is a distant memory, it is completely over. As soon as you have the urge to go to the bathroom, you will wake up immediately and will not wet the bed. You will then get up and go to the bathroom. You are in control.

The main reason you had wet the bed and not woken up in the past is that you have been sleeping too deeply. From now on you will not sleep so deeply, you will sleep lighter than you have before so that when you have the urge to urinate you will realize it immediately and be able to wake up to go to the bathroom. Even though you are not sleeping deeply anymore, you will still receive the rest that your body requires. In fact, you'll find that you will wake up more relaxed and refreshed with the added confidence of knowing that you are in control.

When you wake up in the morning, successful, you will have confidence in your new ability, which will help you to become more and more successful. You feel good about yourself because you are successful. There is no one to blame, and you have done nothing wrong in the past, you have just been sleeping too deeply and that habit has now changed. You are now in control.

Nail Biting

Nail biting is a negative habit that often develops as a way to deal with undesirable stress. Just as with any other bad habit, it must be replaced with a good habit in order to be changed. The new, positive habit that it will be replaced with is relaxation.

You now realize that nail biting is just a way to deal with stress. You have now outgrown that behavior. Now you are informing your subconscious mind, the child within, that biting nails is no longer the way to deal with stress. Now that you are an adult, you want your nails to look healthy and strong. So from this point forward, whenever you have stress, you'll deal with it in a different way. All you need to do is simply take a deep breath and as you exhale, simply say to yourself quietly . . . *relax now* . . . when you do this, you'll find all the stress fades away. Nail biting is part of the past and you do not do it anymore. Your nails and the surrounding skin on your fingers will heal and become healthy once again. Your subconscious mind always wants to help you, and now it will be happy to change and help you to be healthier and happier.

Imagine placing your hands up with your fingers extended outward right in front of you, and now imagine your fingertips and your nails looking exactly like you would like them to look. Visualize them clearly in your mind if you cannot imagine them in front of you. Just think about it and the same purpose is being served. This is what your nails should look like, and will look like.

Your subconscious mind is there every step of the way to help your fingertips heal and be healthy just like you are visualizing them right now. You have developed a new, positive habit of taking a deep breath as a way to deal with stressful situations. You are successful and you will remain successful every step of the way.

Teeth Grinding

Teeth grinding, also known as bruxism, is also a way of dealing with anxiety and stress. Unfortunately, this particular type of event is one that can result in permanent damage to your teeth. Upon eliminating this negative habit, many people also find that they experience fewer headaches as well.

Grinding your teeth is a nervous reaction or vent, which is your body's way of dealing with stress and nervousness in the past and you no longer do it anymore. As of this moment, right now, you no longer grind your teeth. Your new way of dealing with stress is simply taking a deep breath and as you exhale you let all the stress go. Remember, you are in control. Grinding teeth was a negative habit, and you have let it go. Letting it go like a negative thing of the past. You no longer hurt yourself as a way of dealing with stress. You feel confident and happy that you no longer grind your teeth. You will find that your teeth are becoming healthier and your entire mouth feels better.

Things that used to bother you or upset you or stress you no longer affect you anymore. You no longer need a physical outlet or a nervous habit to relieve stress or tension. That negative habit is gone and being replaced with a positive habit. From now on all you need to do is simply take a deep breath and as you exhale, simply say to yourself quietly . . . *relax now* . . . when you do this, you'll find all the stress fades away and everything is fine. You are now in control.

Right Thoughts, Speech, and Actions

Everything in life begins with thought. Your thoughts determine your speech as well as your actions. By practicing the art of correct or right thoughts, speech, and actions, you'll find that you will attract much more positive opportunities into your life.

Positive thinking is very important to you. Positive thinking will bring to you positive results. You now practice the art of right thoughts, speech, and actions. The way you do this is by becoming more sensitive and alert to your thoughts on a daily basis.

The average human being has approximately 64,000 thoughts a day, and to take the time to screen each and every one of those is a full-time job in itself. Rather than taking the time to screen each and every thought, you will now become more aware of your feelings.

Your feelings are the gauge of whether your thought processes are positive or negative. If you are feeling negative or down, chances are you are having negative thoughts. Once you realize that you are having negative thoughts, it is the time to begin correcting your thoughts and especially correcting your speech and actions.

Keep in mind that once you begin having negative thoughts, you will voice those negative thoughts and your resulting actions will be negative as well. By constantly correcting your thoughts and speech, you will have positive actions that will in turn result in positive opportunities for you.

In addition to utilizing your feelings to correct your thoughts, you can also utilize a technique known as thought stopping. The way this works is whenever you notice that you are thinking negative thoughts or whenever you hear negative input coming from any outside source, simply say to yourself out loud the word *stop*. You would then replace the negative input with the correct positive input.

You find that it is easy to keep positive thoughts. Positive thinking is important to you. You enjoy positive thinking because you know it is attracting more positive to you. You realize that it is impossible for positive thoughts to attract negative things. They are two different frequencies.

Whenever you find yourself saying a negative statement, you will change it immediately to a positive one or you will not end it. You will find that each and every day that you are vigilant in monitoring your thought and speech that you will be happier and opportunity will follow you.

Enjoying Life

There are many ways to enjoy life. This script will help you enjoy life from within through happiness, mindfulness, and intention, which will lead you to long-lasting enjoyment.

Take a moment to identify what you desire most in life. What are your goals? What do you feel will truly bring you happiness?

Happiness occurs in the present. The past is gone and the future has not arrived yet.

Happiness is all that you have. Keep in mind that enjoying life is a choice. You can make a choice to be happy, and you can also make a choice to be sad. You choose to be happy. You choose to enjoy each moment of your life.

From this moment forward you find new ways to enjoy your life. Even throughout a day of routine you can enjoy your life more than you ever have if you choose to. All you need to do is to break down each portion of your day, whether it be routine or not, and ask yourself how you can make that portion of your day better.

Take a moment right now and imagine the rest of this day. What will you be doing immediately upon finishing this session? Whatever it is that you will be doing, what can you do to make it better? Seriously consider that question. How can you make it better? Even if it is as simple a task as going to the grocery store, what can you do differently to enjoy life? Perhaps this time you can play your favorite music while you are driving there. Perhaps rather than walking to your vehicle you can run and enjoy the invigoration of exercise. Perhaps at the grocery store you may buy something special just to treat yourself. You may even greet the cashier with an extra warm smile, showing true concern in how she is doing. You may even take the opportunity to help someone struggling with a large package or purchase.

One of the most powerful means of happiness is being of service to others. By being of service to others you are enhancing your own life. By making someone else happy, it makes you happy. By helping someone you are helping yourself. Take the time to think of how you can brighten up someone else's day, whether it be through a simple compliment or actually helping someone in some way.

By making a constant practice of improving the various segments of your day, even if they are mundane segments, you will find that you will enjoy life more than you could have ever dreamed. Enjoy your life . . . enjoy being happy. You have a right to be happy and to enjoy everything that you do.

Improve Relationships

The following script is designed to help you attract positive relationships as well as improve the one you may be in. While trying to improve a relationship, it is vital that you focus on what you want rather than what you want to avoid. This way you are placing your thoughts, focus, and attention on progress.

You have achieved and are on your way to achieving the goals that you set for yourself. You feel strong and confident about yourself. You are comfortable in the direction that you're heading and because of that you do not need to worry about what the future will bring. You feel independent and strong. You know that you are worthwhile. Your personality attracts the right people to you and keeps people interested in you.

You feel at peace within yourself. You're confident and happy about being alive. You feel grateful at this time that you have this great relationship. You don't need to know the future of the relationship, because you are enjoying the now of being with this individual.

You know that the future will be the best it can be so you trust in the way things are working for you. You honor this relationship by staying in the gratitude of being in it and the belief that everything that happens is just right for you.

While in a relationship, you have a desire to improve it, and you realize that one of the most important factors in a great relationship is that it requires two people rather than just one. This means that from this moment forward you no longer think and act simply as an individual, as you may have in the past. You realize that all decisions that you are making from this point forward now involve two people. You now take into consideration what your partner may want and what is in your partner's best interests. You place the happiness of your partner in very high esteem. You are constantly trying to find ways to please and make your partner's life easier.

Sports Focus

The purpose of this script is to increase focus and eliminate distractions. It will help you to be the best at whatever you choose to do.

You have a new, enhanced sense of concentration . . . You are able to block out distractions and concentrate 100 percent on your task at will . . . Your focus is like a laser beam.

You have the energy and strength to be the best at your game . . . You find yourself training harder and improving beyond your expectations . . . You realize that what your mind can conceive, you can and will achieve. You are the best at what you do.

You visualize yourself attaining your goal, being the best, and winning . . . You now have a laser beam focus on your tasks and goals

. . . Nothing takes you away from your goal. Visualize yourself right now in a competition situation . . . See yourself pulling ahead of the rest and excelling in your progress . . . See yourself giving 100 percent of your abilities. You are this winner that you are imagining . . . You are successful . . . You are a winner.

You improve as you give more and more to your training. You are excelling and are the best at your game. Your concern is not only if you will win . . . but how much can you win by. You realize you have no limitations . . . You excel and achieve greatness because you believe in yourself.

Continue to move ahead . . . continue to excel . . . keep your laser beam focus and reach for the GOLD. You are a winner.

Past-Life Regression

The following script can be used for self-hypnosis and also for a group hypnosis session on past-life regression. Keep in mind that in a group session it may be difficult to use a script as each person may experience a different journey. The script is designed for you to answer quietly to yourself when asked questions about what you are experiencing.

Now that you are totally relaxed, I would like you to use your imagination. This entire journey that you will be going through is based solely on your imagination. Therefore, let your mind roam free and allow whatever feelings, thoughts, images, or impressions you have go through your mind. Remember that the subconscious mind, especially when it is concerned with journeying such as in this past-life regression process, operates according to your imagination.

Imagine finding yourself out in the country on a beautiful summer's day . . . You are standing on a path, going through the forest and flowers . . . such a happy, colorful place . . . It seemed just like the ones you read about in fairy tales . . . perfect in every way . . . As you walk down the path you notice that just up ahead is a small bridge going over a babbling brook . . . You go over the bridge and enjoy the beautiful view of the brook and realize that on the other side the path splits off in three directions.

Wherever you choose to go from here, you will be safe and will not experience anything first hand . . . instead, it will be as if you are sitting somewhere, watching your journey unfold in front of you, as if you were sitting in a theater watching yourself on a movie screen . . .

As you approach the three paths, you notice three signs labeling them . . . The one on the right says "past" . . . the center one says "present" . . . and the one on the left says "future" . . . You decide to go to the one on the right and proceed along your journey . . . You notice up ahead that there are smaller paths going off of this main one on either side, each one seeming to disappear into a white blanket of fog . . . You realize that each one of these paths represents a different life that you may have had . . . You decide to walk down the path until you feel one side path is beckoning to you . . . or you just feel that you have a desire to go down one . . . You choose that path and enter the comfortable fog, realizing you are safe . . .

As you emerge on the other side of the fog, you find yourself in a past life . . . Just feel for a few moments all the sensations around you . . . I will be asking the questions, to help you with your journey, and the first thought or impression that comes to mind is the right one . . . Don't try to analyze it or think critically of it, just let it happen . . . So get an idea of where you are now, your surroundings . . . Take in all the feelings, the sensations . . . First of all, where do you think you are right now? . . . Is it light or is it dark? . . . Is it cold or warm? . . . Do you think you are indoors or outdoors? . . . Once again, remember the first impression that comes to you is the right one . . . Get a feel for yourself. Does it seem as though you have anything on your feet? . . . If so what is the texture like . . . what do you think you are wearing? . . . What about clothing? If you have clothing on, describe it as much as you can . . . How tall are you? . . . How old do you think you are? . . . Are you male or female? . . . What color is your hair, if you have any? . . . Your eyes? . . . What are you noticing around you? . . . Are there any landmarks or things that would give you an idea of where you are . . . or maybe even what year it is? . . . Describe your surroundings to yourself in detail . . . If you are outdoors . . . what's there? . . . What can you see? . . . If you can't see much, then walk a little ways to see if you can see more there . . . If you are indoors, describe everything you see . . . If there is not enough for you to get an idea of where you are, then walk over to a window or an opening, somewhere where you can see outside . . . Is there anyone there with you? . . . What do they look like? . . . Describe them . . . Who are they? . . .

Now take a deep breath . . . as deep as you can, and as you exhale just relax completely . . . I want you to feel yourself going ahead a few years now in the same life if you can, all right now stop . . . and wherever you are, get a good feeling for yourself and your surroundings again, and answer to yourself the same kind of questions that I asked you earlier . . . First of all, where are you now? . . . Is it dark or light? . . . Is it cold or warm? . . . Do you think you are indoors or outdoors? . . . Get a feel for yourself . . . Does it seem like you have anything on your feet? . . . What do you think you are wearing?

. . . How about clothing? . . . Describe it as much as you can . . . How tall are you? . . . How old do you think you are? . . . What color is your hair? . . . Your eyes? . . . Who are you? . . . What do you think your purpose is? . . . What is your name? . . . What do people address you by? . . . What are you noticing around you, are there any landmarks or things that would give you an idea where you are? . . . Or maybe what year it is? . . . Where do you live? . . . Imagine your dwelling right in front of you . . . What does it look like? . . . Describe your surroundings to yourself in detail right now . . . If you can't see that much, again, take a little walk to see if you can see more . . . If you are indoors, describe everything there . . . You may even want to walk to a window or an opening to see what is outside . . . Is there anyone here with you? . . . What do they look like? . . . Who are they? . . . Describe their faces . . . Their mouth, hair, eyes . . . Look deeply into their eyes . . . Do they remind you of someone you might know? . . .

Now take a deep breath . . . and exhale . . . I want you to move ahead again, just feel yourself moving ahead in time . . . and I want you to stop approximately a few minutes just before your death scene . . . Whatever you died of . . . remember you will be viewing this as if you are sitting someplace comfortable, watching yourself on a movie screen, so you will feel no discomfort, pain, or anything negative whatsoever . . . You will just be watching it on a screen . . . So bring yourself now to just a few minutes before your death scene . . . Get a feeling for what's going on around you . . . Sensations, sounds, smells . . . What do you see? . . . Where are you? . . . Is there anybody there with you? . . . If so, who are they? . . . What kinds of things are they saying? . . . What are you dying of? . . . Describe yourself wherever you are . . . What do you think is wrong? . . . What kind of thoughts are going through your head right now? . . . Feelings? . . . Is there anyone close to you nearby, a relative, a loved one? . . . Who is it? . . . Once again, describe their faces to yourself, look deeply into their eyes . . . Do you recognize them as anybody you might know in your present life? . . . Do you have any regrets, anything that you feel you might have wanted to do differently? . . . Is there any lesson you can learn, or is there a moral to the life?

Take a deep breath . . . and exhale . . . and imagine a large door of light right in front of you . . . warm, comfortable, inviting light . . . Go ahead and step through the light now leaving that life behind . . . As you step through the light, you are coming to a comfortable, relaxing, wonderful place.

You turn away with your back to the light and you see that path in front of you once again you came down initially, and you go back down that path heading back to the present time and place . . . walking down the path going back to the bridge . . . As you go back down the path through that other door of light . . . that you initially came through . . . walking through the door of light, you come out on the other side . . . and you feel yourself coming back to the present day and time, to the present date, feeling wonderful and refreshed from the journey.

Chapter 13
Education and Learning

The following scripts in this chapter are designed to help students of all ages to excel in all areas of education. There are scripts that can help you with study habits, test taking, gaining confidence, problem solving, and even how to stop sabotaging yourself so you can attain your goals.

Eliminate Self-Sabotage

Self-sabotage is a negative occurrence that can happen to you without you even realizing it. In the course of attaining your goals, it is easy to hinder your own progression. If you have ever found that you had destructive behaviors that stood in the way of your expectations, you should consider listening to this script on self-sabotage.

You are now highly motivated. You exude confidence in all that you do. Self-doubt and fear are things of the past, and you now replace them with confidence and conviction. You trust your abilities and know that you can do anything that you set your mind on. You are successful in all that you do. Other people enjoy being around you because of your confidence and ability. You have a very open mind and are creative.

You are your own best friend and can accomplish anything you wish. You are a self-confident, successful winner who accomplishes your goals. Your only limitation is your imagination, and now you let your imagination run free. You are a winner, your life is a series of successes.

You allow only positive thoughts to run through your mind. You have a strong drive to be successful, to be a winner. Any task that you take on, you are confident and have a strong sense of follow-through. You finish all tasks in a positive manner and never have any doubt that you will succeed.

Your new motto is, Do it now! You are going to find that beginning right now you are success oriented. You expect to succeed in everything. You feel enthusiasm and confidence in all that you do. From now on you no longer procrastinate. You feel a sense of urgency to complete all that needs to be done. You feel a sense of satisfaction as you accomplish more and more each day. Every day your work gets easier to accomplish, to finish.

You are going to become a doer rather than a worrier. You know that you will do your best, and your best will become better and better. You'll do it now! By leaving procrastination behind you are going to find that you have more time to do the things that you enjoy. You'll feel more organized, more in control, more confident. You'll find that your free time is indeed just that, your free time!

No More Excuses

By eliminating excuses you are taking 100 percent responsibility for your life. This script will help you to take control of your life by identifying and eliminating excuses that you may have allowed to stand in your way.

From this point forward you are taking responsibility for your own actions . . . You are no longer making excuses for your actions or placing blame with anyone else . . . You take responsibility . . . You are becoming truthful with yourself . . . especially in the area of your actions . . . You own them . . . You alone are responsible for what you do . . . whether you are experiencing happiness or difficulties with your life . . . You now realize that they come from you.

You are now able to look inside . . . to go beyond the surface . . . and then even a little bit further . . . By looking deep inside yourself . . . and becoming honest with yourself . . . You realize that you no longer have to rationalize . . . or make excuses . . . for the occurrences of things that happen in your life.

You realize that in order to change anything in your life . . . that change begins with you . . . You realize that by being honest, and facing the truth about yourself . . . that only then can change take place . . . You realize that who you are today is a direct result of the decisions that you made yesterday . . . and who you will be tomorrow will depend on the decisions that you make today.

You now identify the things that make you upset or frustrated . . . Once you have found these things, you are able to change them . . . and in so doing you can progress.

From this moment forward . . . these are the new, life-changing steps that you embrace willingly and happily . . . to find happiness in your life . . . You now take the time and effort to examine yourself by looking inside . . . You face the truth about yourself and your actions . . . You take responsibility for your actions . . . You no longer make excuses . . . You do not blame any other person, such as parents, friends, or even society, for your situations or your actions . . . You are in control . . . and responsible for your own destiny.

Enhance Concentration

Once you are able to concentrate more on the tasks you are working on, you'll be able to do them better. Concentrating will help you improve in all areas of your life. Being able to concentrate better will also instill more confidence in you.

Your mind is the most perfect computer in existence, and now your computer is able to concentrate better than before, and this new ability will stay with you because you have interest in what you're now doing . . . because you can focus totally on what is before you.

Feel the confidence that you now have being in control . . . Feel the confidence that you now have that you can attain your goals . . . that you can concentrate . . . that you now enjoy what you are doing . . . Allow this confidence to surge throughout your body . . . and to grow as you feel it expand to every part of you . . . Feeling wonderful in every way . . . that you are a success . . . and that you will be successful in all that you do.

You are calm, relaxed, and in control. From this moment on you are able to concentrate, infinitely better than ever before. You are able to concentrate and focus better because you are giving it 100 percent of your attention. Whatever task you are doing, you now give it 100 percent of your attention, by doing so you find it more interesting and enjoyable. You find all your studies or projects interesting and you are able to concentrate so much more easily. Your new ability to concentrate better allows you to remember what it is you are studying or learning.

You now have 100 percent concentration in any area that you desire because you choose to. You are able to filter out distractions upon command. You are able to bring yourself to the now, realizing that all that exists is this very moment. Knowing this, you are able to filter out negativity from the past as well as expectations of the future so that you can focus on the now. You are in control.

Stress-Free Test Taking

When preparing for a test, all of the information that you are studying is being stored in your subconscious mind. If you have taken the time to prepare for your test, the information that you require is stored in your subconscious mind. Keep in mind that the purpose of a test is simply for your instructor to ensure that you know the information that has been taught. If you know the information, there is no reason for stress or anxiety. All you need to do is show what you know.

Right now, you are changing the way you look at test taking. You have come to this deep, relaxed state so as to learn an effective way to take tests successfully. Let every negative thought from the past having to do with taking tests go away. Let all negativity fade away like an old memory that is not useful to you anymore because right now . . . you are going to learn the most effective techniques for taking tests. From this moment on you will look forward to test taking and will do very well with them.

One of the secrets of test taking is simply to know what your instructor is asking. All test taking is . . . a way for you to show how well you have learned your materials and how well you have studied, and from now on you will do very well in taking tests because you will be prepared for them.

You will find that all of your studies come easily to you because you enjoy what you are studying. You now study for your tests at the earliest convenience and you are able to retain all that you read. Remembering is not an effort for you. All information that you study, read, or take in from any of your senses is recorded in your subconscious mind. It is the world's best computer, and you now have the ability to recall information at will.

When you are taking a test, you look forward to taking it because you know your subject matter, you have studied, and are anxious to show how well you know it. You are always relaxed when you take your tests and information comes to you easily. As soon as you read the questions on your test, the answer immediately comes to you. It is clear as a bell and there is no confusion. If you find yourself getting anxious during the test or are not remembering immediately, you will simply take a deep breath and relax and the answer will flow through your mind freely.

You no longer second-guess yourself, as the answers will immediately come to you. Test taking is easy . . . Test taking is enjoyable and exciting . . . You are prepared. Congratulations on your success.

Heighten Memory Retention

In order to access the portion of the mind where memories are stored, it is imperative to relax. It is similar to placing everything you have studied all around you and then upon taking a test you decide to put blinders on your face such as the ones that are used on a horse. Now you can only see in front of you even though all the information that you studied is still all around you. By relaxing you are able to remove these blinders.

All information that you have ever seen, heard, or felt since the day you were born is stored in your subconscious mind . . . Every thought, sound, sight, taste, and even smell is logged in perfect clarity. Your subconscious mind is more powerful than the strongest computer ever made and it is available to you . . . at will . . . if you desire it . . . All you need to do is relax . . . and let go . . .

Each and everything that is important for you to remember you do with complete ease. You recall exactly what you need, when you need it, effortlessly and easily. Everything you need to know is committed to your memory and you are able to retrieve it spontaneously as the situation demands. As you remember more and more important information, you grow confident in your memory's ability.

The more you relax, the more you are able to retrieve anything that you like. So from now on, whenever you need to remember something, all that you need to do is to simply sit back, take a deep breath, and relax . . . knowing that the answer will come to you . . . and it will. Have the confidence that your answers or whatever you need to remember are in your subconscious mind. Have the confidence that you can retrieve anything, allow yourself to relax and it will come.

You now have total recall at will . . . Remembering is now a priority for you . . . and it is easy and natural for you to remember . . . It doesn't have to be difficult to be worthwhile . . . It can be very simple . . . What you need to remember is easy to remember. As you receive new information, you have total recall of this information at will . . . you now have the ability to retrieve that information whenever you like.

Improve Study Habits

One of the key features in the art of studying is to be interested in what you are learning. Even if it is a topic that you feel you may not be able to use in the future, you'll find that by showing interest in it you will absorb so much more.

You have continued to study the same way since you were a child. As you grew older many things in your life have changed; however, you are still studying the same way. So you will now learn a more effective, better way of studying. Setting a new habit is easy to do, and you are now going to set a new habit of studying.

Your mind is the most perfect computer ever made. Your strong subconscious mind stores every bit of information that you have ever experienced. All that information and all the new information that you are now learning is available with perfect recall in your mind. You retain all the information that you learn.

You now find all of your studies interesting, and because you find them interesting you'll find it very easy to concentrate on your studies. You will not become bored with your studies because you find them so interesting. You enjoy learning new information. You find that you now absorb all information that you learn.

You no longer procrastinate or put off your studies because you find your studies so interesting. You will get them done as early as possible. By doing this you'll find that you have more free time. It gives you a great sense of confidence and satisfaction to finish and be caught up on all of your studies. You find that you are more disciplined in your studies than ever before.

Boost Confidence

Confidence is a topic that can be addressed using self-hypnosis sessions. It is something that many people don't have enough of and many can use more of. The following script will help you fill this void.

You are a confident person. You are in control in all that you do. You believe in yourself and in your abilities. You are successful in all areas of your life. Believing in yourself and being positive gives you the confidence that you desire.

When attempting something new, the first thing that comes into your mind are the words "I can do it." You realize that what your mind can conceive your mind can achieve, and you move forward with all things. You are open-minded and move ahead with confidence that you can and will succeed. You are a winner, you are confident, and you are in control.

You are in control of all aspects of your life now. You notice yourself becoming more confident and more in control than ever before. You notice every day that your attitude is becoming more cheerful and free of concern about life's daily problems. You will direct your mind to drift to positive, happy, constructive thoughts. You are in control.

You will feel positive that everything in life will work out for you. You are becoming more aware everyday of an inner peace and calmness that will give you more control over all aspects of your life.

Your mind is now calm and focused . . . you enjoy your peaceful and happy experiences. Your self-esteem is increasing . . . and you are enjoying your newfound confidence. You can now focus on the task at hand, and feel good about yourself. You are enthusiastic about your new life . . .

You see yourself as a responsible, important person. You no longer worry about situations that you cannot control . . . you enjoy your ability to focus . . . you like being in control. You are confident, focused, and determined . . . You are happy with who you are.

Gain Self-Esteem

Self-esteem is a very important factor in your personal development. The way that you see yourself is the way that you portray yourself to others. The following script will help you improve your self-esteem, which will help you improve your relationships with others.

You have come to this very relaxed state to feel better about yourself and your abilities. Beginning right now, you will realize and accept that you are a worthwhile and lovable person. You will react to others with the conviction and confidence that they will accept you in a positive way.

From this day forward, when you look into the mirror you will see a confident and capable person . . . all the negative statements that you may have heard in your past are no more . . . In fact, anytime someone says something negative to you, your subconscious mind will cancel the statement and not accept it . . . You deserve happiness . . . You are a unique and beautiful being . . . You have talents and gifts that no other person has . . . Success and happiness are your birthright . . . From this day forward you will be self-confident . . . capable and determined . . . You love yourself . . . You are an important and valuable person . . .

You will be happy and confident in your ability to complete tasks with greater focus . . . with honesty and fairness . . . and in a timely manner. You will appreciate how others have faith in you and respect your abilities. You will no longer feel threatened by things in your life that need changing. You will be able to accomplish these changes with positive planning.

You will feel happy, worthwhile, and able to be loved and confident. You will notice how people react to you with respect and acceptance and know that as you love yourself, love the person that you are, others will see the very same things in you that you now see in yourself.

Excel at Problem Solving

This script will help you solve problems by looking at them as challenges and taking the time to reflect on them. By relaxing and keeping an open mind, many times the elusive solution to a problem is right in front of you. This session will help you to be open to possibilities.

You are now very creative when approaching problem solving. You now look at problems as challenges and are excited to find their solutions. By being creative and allowing your mind to relax and be comfortable, you will find that answers will come to you that will suit your needs. When trying to find a solution . . . you now take a deep breath . . . relax . . . and examine the challenge.

People seem to look everywhere else for a solution when the answer is sitting right in front of you. Be attentive and open-minded and your strong subconscious will guide you. Be sensitive to your inner feelings.

Do not be afraid to think outside the box. Your answer may come in a totally different way or thought process. Allow your mind to be open to all possibilities no matter how outrageous they may initially sound. Patience is a virtue.

Think about your concerns when you go to sleep, giving your strong subconscious time to work on it while you are sleeping. Be open-minded and optimistic. Many times you will wake up in the morning with the answer.

Asking advice or getting a second opinion from a peer is a sign of wisdom and maturity. Do not look at it as a sign of weakness. Oftentimes someone outside of the situation or problem can easily see the solution that may have been elusive to you.

Chapter 14
What's Next?

You now have the knowledge and tools at your fingertips to successfully accomplish many of your goals. You also have the knowledge to help many of your friends and family with their health, success, and happiness. There are so many choices available to you. This is the beginning of a new you.

You're a Self-Hypnotist

You have now joined the ranks of the self-enlightened. You know the procedure for utilizing your subconscious mind to attain your goals. Keep in mind that knowledge alone is simply unused potential. In order for the knowledge to become power, it must be acted upon.

Rather than trying to do everything all at once, take the time to organize your thoughts into a plan. Of all the topics that you now have available to you, separate out the three that are the most important. Once you have chosen them, decide which one you would like to do first.

 Alert!

You will have better success in approaching goals one at a time. Keep in mind that the subconscious is similar to a four-year-old child. If you ask a child to do seven major tasks all at once, he would become overwhelmed and likely quit altogether. It is best to accomplish one task completely and then move on to the next.

Once you have targeted the issues that you would like to improve upon, take time to create a plan for how you will approach it. You have many variations available on how to conduct self-hypnosis. Choose the vehicle that will best suit your lifestyle. Decide if there is a script that will be suitable to your needs or whether you should create your own. Once you have created your plan, it is important to make a commitment to follow through until completion in order to be successful.

Future Plans

In addition to the many ways that you can help yourself with self-hypnosis, you now have many other options. You may decide to simply use hypnosis to help yourself and others close to you as a hobby, or you may decide to take it much further. There are many options available to you.

While you are taking the time to plan what you would like to do with this information, try to begin a daily self-improvement regimen. It is important that the information is fresh in your mind and that you begin to use it and continue to do so until it becomes comfortable to you. Simply listening to a short relaxation self-hypnosis session on a daily basis can do wonders for you.

 Essential

As you take the time to create your goals, write them down and be as specific as possible. The act of writing things down is significant in the creative thought process. Writing down your goals will be the difference between having an attainable, detailed goal or a wishful thought.

Choices, Choices, Choices

No matter what you decide to do, it always boils down to choices. Being successful or not is a choice, being happy or sad is a choice, and even having a wonderful relation-ship is a choice.

Making a choice requires taking action, and virtu-ally all of the choices you will be required to make if you decide to progress will require change. Change is incon-venient because it means you will have to do something different than you have been doing. Whatever it is that you decide to do, remember that taking action means to do it now.

 Fact

> Due to the extreme relaxation benefits of self-hyp-nosis, each fifteen minutes of hypnosis is similar to receiving approximately four hours of sleep. If you find yourself tired throughout the day without time for a nap, a short fifteen-minute session can greatly rejuvenate you.

Change requires you to shake up your life and go against your natural desires. Remember, it is the nature of the conscious mind to remain the same. It rebels against change, and you must be aware of this rebel-lion as you attain your goals. Your own conscious mind may try to stop you; however, you are in control at all times. Be persistent with your self-hypnosis so you can bypass this temporary self-sabotaging, and you will be successful.

What Can You Do Now?

There are many things that you can do with this new knowledge that you acquired in addition to helping yourself and your loved ones with their path to self-improvement. Following are just a few of the paths that you may choose to take.

Become a Professional Hypnotist

You may decide to start a part-time business as a hypnotist, helping others with important issues such as smoking cessation, stress reduction, and weight loss. You may even decide to take further training to become a certified hypnotherapist and start your own full-time business. There are many schools available on the Internet as well as wonderful home study courses that can teach you all you need to know to get started.

Life Coaching or Hypno-Counseling

Life coaching and counseling have become very popular, and there are many courses available that will easily teach you to be effective in these fields. Conducting them in conjunction with hypnosis makes them even more effective.

Become a Comedy Hypnotist

Perhaps you would be more interested in a lucrative career that is not only interesting but very entertaining as well. Comedy hypnosis is growing by leaps and bounds especially in colleges and high schools across America. There is also a great call for comedy hypnotists in comedy clubs, fairs, festivals, corporate outings, and even on cruise ships.

Clean Slate of Awareness

One of the most wonderful things about life is that every morning you can start a brand new day. Everyone in this world, whether they are successful or not, has the same twenty-four hours in a day. The key to success is how you use them.

It's as if each and every day you are given a second chance to make of your life whatever you want. Each new day you have a clean slate. The past is gone, you are living in the present, and the future is wide open.

 Essential

> Many people find it difficult to determine what their exact goals are. If you're stuck, create a list of everything you do not want. Then on a parallel column write the exact opposite of each item you had written. By doing this you will be surprised with what you came up with.

The Unwritten Chapter

Imagine yourself reading a book that has been written about your life from the day you were born up to this moment. When you turn the page to read what happens to you an hour from now, you find that the page is blank.

In other words, you can put whatever you would like to happen on this new, blank page.

The choice is yours whether tomorrow morning will be just like yesterday or if it will be completely different. In this unwritten chapter you have the opportunity to do or be anything your mind can conceive.

We all have the same opportunities in life. Although everyone's past may have been different, from this moment forward we are all confronting a blank page. Keep in mind that no matter what your goal might be, if someone else has done it, so can you. If someone else has done it, it is possible. By studying that person, then attaining the same knowledge required and following their same steps, logic states that you should also be able to attain their same result.

What will you write in your book? How far will you allow your newfound talents of self-hypnosis to propel you? Remember, everything that you do or don't do in life is a choice. Make a choice to move forward.

Appendix A
Glossary

age progression:
Advancing the subject's age level while in hypnosis.

age regression:
Acting out past events in the framework of the present. A re-experiencing of earlier events in life usually limited to a specific time or time period.

amnesia:
The loss of memory.

analgesia:
Feeling pressure but no pain, also known as glove anesthesia.

anesthesia:
Insensibility to feelings of physical pain.

anxiety:
A painful uneasiness of mind.

authoritative:
Parental, forceful, strong, domineering, direct.

autoconditioning:
A series of experiments designed to bring one's subconscious under control.

autohypnosis:
Self-hypnosis.

autosuggestion:
Self-suggestions; self-talk.

catalepsy:
A condition characterized by a rigidity of the skeletal muscles.

clinical hypnosis:
The therapeutic use of hypnosis.

compounding:
If one thing that is stated happens, then the next must also be true.

conditioning:
A series of inductions making certain ideas or things acceptable to the subject's subconscious mind.

conscious:
Being aware of an inward state or an outside fact.

contention:
Attention with a little concentration, without effort.

Couéism:
The principles of autosuggestion as advocated by Émile Coué. ("Every day in every way, I am getting better and better.")

delusion:
An irrational belief held in spite of all evidence to the contrary.

dissociation:
The separation of consciousness of certain mental processes that function independently.

expectancy:
Believing in the positive results. A firm belief or a vague feeling that this thing you want will happen.

facilitation:
The acceptance of one suggestion always aids in the acceptance of another. The persuasive salesperson who forces the prospect to answer many unimportant questions with yes before popping the big one is using facilitation.

fixation:
In this stage, the subject is literally hanging on every word said by the operator.

forensic hypnosis:
Using hypnosis to uncover the truth or lost information. Legal application of hypnosis.

free association:
Spontaneous, unrestricted associations of loosely linked ideas or mental images having very little rational sequence or continuity.

grading:
The ranking of suggestions from low to high difficulty. Easy suggestions come before hard ones.

hallucinations:
Seeing something that is not there; similar to a mirage.

hypersuggestibility:
The capacity to easily respond to suggestions.

hypnagogic:
The intermediate state between wakefulness and sleep.

hypnosis:
From the Greek word for *sleep*. Being open to suggestion. There are many vehicles to achieve this state, including relaxation, confusion, and the use of medication.

hypnotherapy:
Any therapy in which the use of hypnosis is utilized.

hypnotic:
Pertaining to or associated with hypnotism.

hypnotic passes:
Gestures or movements made by the hypnotist over the body of the subject without actually touching the subject.

hypnotism:
The science of hypnosis.

hypnotist:
The operator conducting the hypnosis session.

hypnotizability:
An individual's susceptibility to hypnosis.

hypnotize:
The act of inducing a hypnotic state.

ideomotor action/response:
The involuntary response of muscles to thoughts, feelings, and ideas rather than a sensory stimulus.

imagery:
The ability to perceive or mentally recreate ideas, pictures, or feelings.

indirect hypnosis:
The production of hypnosis without the subject's awareness.

induction:
The production of hypnosis through the use of specific procedures.

lay hypnotist:
Anyone practicing hypnosis outside of the medical profession.

mass hypnosis:
Simultaneous induction of a large group,

mnemonic:
Something that assists memory; an aid for remembering.

monoideism:
Term coined by Scottish physician James Braid, who also first introduced the term *hypnosis*, for waking hypnosis and light stages of hypnosis.

negative hallucination:
Not seeing something that is there. For example, the clock on the wall becomes invisible.

objectivity:
Ability to view events, ideas, and phenomena as external and apart from self-consciousness; detached and impersonal.

operator:
A hypnotist; the person conducting a hypnosis session.

permissive:
Soft-spoken; nondirective yet persuasive.

phobia:
A strong, irrational fear.

posthypnotic suggestion:
Suggestions made during the hypnotic state to be carried out after awakening.

projection:
Attributing one's own feelings to someone else.

psychosomatic:
Functional interrelationship between mind and body.

pyramiding of suggestions:
Each successful challenge guarantees the success of the next, more difficult challenge, from simple test to difficult test.

rapport:
Relation of harmony, comfort, and accord; state of being in tune with your subject.

reality:
True state of anything.

revivification:
Reliving a prior period of life.

rigidity:
Muscle tenseness.

self-control:
Conscious autosuggestion.

self-hypnosis:
Placing one's self into a hypnotic state.

skeptic:
One who doubts or disbelieves.

sleep hypnosis:
Hypnosis brought about while an individual is sleeping, bringing them out of sleep just enough to be in the state between sleep

and wakefulness, the state of suggestibility. Usually conducted on small children with great success.

somnambulism:
In everyday usage, the term connotes sleepwalking; however, in the lexicon of hypnosis, somnambulism is used to designate the deepest state of hypnosis.

somnambulistic state:
A state of the most profound relaxation and usually the hypnotist's objective with a subject. Similar to the sleepwalking state.

subconscious:
The nature of mental operation not yet present in the consciousness.

subject:
The person being hypnotized.

suggestibility:
The capacity to be open to suggestions.

suggestion:
An idea that is offered to the subject for acceptance.

susceptibility:
The capability of receiving impressions.

therapeutic:
Of or pertaining to the healing arts.

time distortion:
A subject's unexplainable lapse of time during hypnosis.

trance:
A supposed state of profound abstraction made popular by the media. There actually is no such state.

unconscious mind:
A term used in psychiatry to denote a postulated region of the psyche, the repository of repressed urges and wishes, often used as a synonym for the *unconscious*.

waking hypnosis:
Hypnotic suggestions accepted by the subject in the waking state.

Appendix B
Frequently Asked Questions

Who can be hypnotized?

Anyone with reasonable intelligence can be hypnotized. The only ones who may not be able to be hypnotized are people with severe mental disability and children under the age of five, because they may not understand the words you are saying or be able to follow your instructions. If you are able to read a book and follow simple instructions, you are hypnotizable, but only if you want to be.

Am I sleeping while under hypnosis?

You are wide awake. You are very aware under hypnosis. You are actually in a state of hypersensitivity. All of your senses and emotions are enhanced. It is closer to a state of daydreaming or relaxing. You are focused on the words of the hypnotherapist and outside sounds will seem to fade away.

Can I get stuck in hypnosis?

No, the hypnotic state can be terminated at any time you chose. It is your choice to enter the state, and you can always choose to leave it. If you were left in a hypnotic state by your hypnotherapist or by a hypnotic tape, you would either return to full consciousness on your own or enter a natural sleep and awaken after a short pleasant nap. There is no trance and you are not under anyone's power.

Will I reveal any deep, dark secrets while under hypnosis?

Not unless you want to. It is not a truth serum! In fact, there are many that say that you can even pass a lie detector test under hypnosis.

Is hypnosis dangerous, and are there any unwanted side effects?

Hypnosis is no more dangerous than sitting in a recliner watching television. You are only using the natural power of your own mind to relieve symptoms and alter unwanted behavior patterns. Hypnotherapy is nonaddictive and safe, and there are no unwanted or unpleasant side effects. The only side effect is feeling very relaxed afterward. Every fifteen minutes of hypnosis is equal to approximately four hours of sleep.

Will I be in control and aware of what is happening?

Yes, you do not go out of control, you are not put under a spell, and you do not go to sleep. You are not unconscious. You are in a state of openness and suggestibility. You can hear everything that is being said. Nothing happens without your consent. You have absolute control; however, you are extremely relaxed.

Is hypnosis suitable for children?

Yes, usually from about the age of five, provided they can understand what is being said and they are intelligent and imaginative. Younger children can benefit from the relaxation. For children under the age of six, sleep hypnosis can be conducted with great success.

Will I do anything against my will?

No, you will not do anything that you do not think is acceptable or against your nature. You cannot be made to violate your own values or accepted patterns of behavior. You would either reject the suggestion or come out of the hypnosis. You will hear everything that is said. You are in complete control at all times.

What is self-image and why is it so important?

How you see yourself on the inside reflects what you become on the outside, your self-image. You are the way you are now because of your memories. Your memories, past experiences, successes, failures, humiliations, and triumphs have given you the self-image that you have now. You can never really rise above your self-image.

Will hypnosis work for me?

Hypnosis will work for you if you have a sincere desire to change, are open-minded, and give 100 percent effort.

What does hypnosis feel like?

You have most likely felt what it is like to be under hypnosis many times. It most closely resembles daydreaming. You may have also been in hypnosis if you have ever come home from a long day's work, sat down on your recliner to relax, and were so relaxed that when someone spoke to you you heard them but they were incoherent. That is what hypnosis feels like to most people.

Index

Printed in the United States
By Bookmasters